Securing Death

Victorious Tears

Securing Death

Dr. Njeri Kamaku

MN

Disclaimer
This book is purely a work of fiction and a product of the author's imagination. Any resemblance to events, names and characters of people, living or dead or places in the real world is purely coincidental and not intentional.

Dedication

To those who seek justice and fair service commensurate to what they pay for and those who seek a better society.

Everything was going south in the country and it seemed like everyone was on the brink of death, not of natural causes but death by design. Corruption had sucked out all the funds meant for services to the citizens... The wastage in the country was leading to so much suffering.

*　　*　　*

"Your wife was expecting a child. She should have been attended the first moment she arrived here and the hospital should have looked for ways of recovering its bills after they had done their work. . . It was better when everyone received their medical allowance, they would choose the cover to take.

*　　*　　*

He went to three hospitals before he decided to go to the only hospital in town which would accept his card. ... they could not carry out some of the tests claiming that they were not covered in his package.

*　　*　　*

He often heard stories of misdiagnoses and medical negligence, but he had not been aware they were of such grave magnitude until he took his wife to the hospital. He remembered the story of his colleague who had had a wrong tooth extracted.

*　　*　　*

The insurance company that had made it hard for her to get treatment gave him a last sendoff cover that was more than enough to cover for all the tests the hospital had refused to carry out because he could not pay the necessary deposit.

Chapter One

He tried to pull the cover to stop the biting cold from gnawing him and at least allow him some few minutes of the sweet sleep but it did not work. It was as if someone was pulling the cover off him and exposing his legs to the elements of the night such as the cold wind that was stealing the comfort of his rest. The cover was getting shorter as if the thief was taking a part of it every second threatening to take it all ultimately. He curved himself, pulling his legs close to the chest but it did not work. As he struggled to hold on to the drowning sleep, it slipped away from him and a fearful presence engulfed him. His heart started beating heavily and he started shivering pulling the cover the more. He would have a busy day on light break.

Johnstone Kahiga, that was the name his parents gave him. They said that he would live as long as a stone, though he often wondered; due to the life he was living, whether it would be a lifeless existence just like the stone outside his house. He regretted the day he became an adult. He remembered how eager he was to become a tall and big person when he was five years. He could not wait for the honor of commanding the respect of everyone that came with it.

He never knew then that it came with so many responsibilities that would demand so much from him. He also did not know there would be robbers who would take away from him what he painfully worked for and there was nothing he could do about it. What was more, he would hardly benefit from whatever they were taking from him with a claim that he was securing his health and future. Every minute he lived, he felt that every subscription he made pointed towards securing his death and that of his family members.

When the twisted cover could not give him the warmth he needed, he sat up on the bed, switched on the lights and stretched his long freezing legs. They were hairy and thin, and long like two poles of flagposts.

"I wonder how long they are going to carry me," he said to himself as he moved towards a table near the bed.

He was wearing a pair of shorts and had no shirt. He pulled on a drawer and removed a photo of a smiling woman. He looked at it and moved his fingers across the lips and the face like he was stroking it.

"How long are you going to stay there? You should know what they are saying and get out of there. When the quota is exhausted, and it seems it has, we will be forced to sell everything we have. Where do you think we will go then?" he asked as a tear dropped from his eye.

He wiped it, placed the photo back in the drawer and pulled an apron to cover himself. He moved to the next room where three of his children were sleeping. He just wanted to check on them but did not want to wake them up. As he groped in the darkness of the room, he knocked down a stool dropping bottles of syrup that lay on top of it. Two of the bottles broke and he had no option but to switch on the lights against his wish.

"How foolish of me. It seems I am going, or rather, everything is breaking on me," he cursed.

He cleaned the syrup on the floor as he looked at the innocent children sleeping without a care in the world, placing their legs on each other. One had his foot inside the mouth of his sister. He moved them, avoiding to deter them from their sleep and after wiping the spilled medicine from the floor, he went back to his room to think.

It was three in the morning. He was meeting the area member of parliament at nine to request him to become a guest of honor in a fundraiser he was preparing to pay for some procedures at the hospital that his scheme could not cover for a reason he could not explain. He could not sleep as he thought about all these things.

He left the bed at five and went to the detached kitchen a few meters from the main house. He had to make breakfast for his children who were still sleeping in their room. He was a bit relaxed that he would not be going to work that day. The schools had closed the previous week. The eldest child would have to take care of the rest and give them food on time, food he was going to prepare that morning before he left. He had come to realize how significant his wife was and the kind of work she did. As it were, he was feeling like he would break down any moment if things did not change soon.

It took him about fifteen minutes to light the fire, a trend he had taken since he took Jennifer to hospital. He regretted all the days he had taken the lady for granted. He had begun to realize how important she was. In fact, he started to appreciate the value of women in life.

That was not the end of his woes, he tried locating a clean pot in the kitchen but could not trace one. The fire went out before he cleaned one that seemed not to heed to his efforts. He lighted it again, this time in seven minutes and placed the pot half filled with water on the fire. Traces of vegetables from the previous night's meal could be seen in the water that he intended to use for tea, some of it stuck stubbornly on the sides of the pot. He added some milk to it to block the eye shore and some floated as if to mock him.

He went outside to sit on the stone that had become the mark of his home. As he sat thinking what life had in store for his family, he imagined many like him who were on the brink of poverty trying to make invisible ends meet while challenges smothered them. He also visualized those who were controlling power getting to eat the fattest parts of the meat of the animal that they were working hard to fatten, as if some had been called to make it fat while others were called to eat of their hard work.

"When will this situation change?" he asked himself as the first light cleared the darkness that covered the land.

He was aroused from his thoughts by the smell of something that was burning. His tea had once again spilled onto the fire, remaining only about three quarters of what he had cooked. He had learned to add more water to his tea to make enough, but that did not go well with the children.

"Your tea is not as tasty as the one mother makes," his younger child had told him one morning.

"Drink your tea and stop complaining," he warned sternly.

"It is true dad, you should add some more milk. This tea you have made looks like milk flew past it and colored it to make it look like milk tea," the elder one teased.

The man was at a loss and missed Jennifer even the more. Why was life so cruel? Just at the moment he had started being in good terms with the love of his life and they were even expecting another child, then disaster had struck. He wondered how he would live if anything happened to her.

He rushed to the kitchen and poured the tea in a vacuum flask without sieving it. The children would know what to do when they woke up. Then he remembered that he had not even bought bread the previous evening. There was nothing in the kitchen to take the tea with. He removed one hundred shillings note from his pocket and placed it under the thermos. He would have left by the time the children woke up. He did not want to miss his appointment with the member of parliament. He hoped the children would realize what the money was meant for. Then he remembered that he had not even cooked the meal for the day. No! They would buy some snacks and wait for him when he came in the evening. He would carry some take away meal from the restaurant in town.

*　　*　　*

Jennifer had just woken up to prepare breakfast for the family and warm water for her husband. She was six months pregnant and was feeling weak. She wondered why her man could not consider her state and help her in some of the house chores. She was not asking him to do everything, but he should at least assist her for that time. He was a man who absolutely believed in traditional gender roles and even if she was crawling, she would have to do her chores and serve her husband.

"Why is the society so unfair to women?" she asked as she drew water from a tank outside the house.

A sharp pain struck her and she held her head. She sat on a rock outside the house holding her head. She could not scream and the child in her womb seemed to have sensed the pain and it became unsettled. She passed out a few minutes later.

"Mama Karangi, is the water not yet ready?" Johnstone called from the bed.

It was getting late and he would be late for work. He was angry at the new headteacher who had been sent to his school. She always reprimanded him for getting late for his first lessons. He projected his anger on his wife but he had not been hard on her for some months. They had been getting along well and were even planning things together.

"Do you want me to get late again and be reprimanded by that woman?" he asked angrily while still on the bed.

Ten minutes had already passed since he asked about the water. His anger rose and he tied a towel on his waist and rushed outside shouting at her.

"For how long am I going to ask for this water? Can't you ever do anything right in this home?"

He opened the door violently and rushed to the kitchen. No one was in the kitchen. He started to panic but kept his cool. He did not shout anymore. So much was going on in his mind. He was angry that his employer had decided to take part of his salary, or rather, to take away from his slip the medical allowance for a health scheme that he did not understand. He had been doing well and was content that he was contributing to the national health scheme, even though he did not get the value he thought he should get for the money he was contributing.

"Where are you now?" he asked calmly when he realized she had not even lit the fire.

Had she got angry with him and ran away? He had not quarreled with her for quite some time. He could therefore not understand what had made her angry. He had realized that she had started getting lazy and many things in the house remained undone. Though he did not say a thing, he was planning to reprimand her for that. He would not entertain a lazy woman in his house. What would his friends say if they realized what was happening? He would not allow anyone to play with his manhood.

"Mama Karangi, if I get late to work, you are all going to leave this house. I cannot stay in a house where nothing gets done. Kahiga doesn't tolerate such," he said as he walked out of the kitchen.

He noticed her lying by the stone that had become the mark of his home. He looked at her and was thinking to use the advice of his friend to restore order in his family.

"I think Damien was right, one cannot stay with these beings without disciplining them. They are no different from children," he said approaching her.

When he reached where she was, he realized that she was not even conscious. What was happening to her? He bent down to lift her but she was too heavy for him. He had not realized that she had grown big and that her weakness and recent laziness was on account of what was happening in her body. He had neglected her.

"What is wrong, Jennifer?" he used the name for the first time in a very long time.

Jennifer did not respond. He quickly rushed to his house and called his brother for help. As he waited for his brother, he wrote a text to his headteacher informing her that he had been in an emergency. He did not wait to get her reply and only got to view it later that evening after he had taken his wife to hospital.

The struggles of the day made him wonder if he was a refugee in his own country. Her reply was nothing any man could laugh about. He felt that the slaves he taught his students about were ten times better off. Then the hospital. It was as if they waited to show him their power and mock him for choosing to become a civil servant, and worse, a teacher.

"We can't treat her unless you give a deposit of fifty thousand shillings. And be careful, her child and she might be in danger," the admitting nurse said as he advised him to hasten.

"Where in the world do you expect me to get all that money? What is the purpose of the insurance scheme if it cannot help me in times like this?" he asked getting frustrated.

"As I informed you, we have suspended the services of your scheme until further notice," the nurse said.

"So, you want her to suspend her sickness until they restore the services?" Johnstone asked angrily.

"You do not have to be rude, I am just doing my work," the nurse said and left them.

Johnstone looked at Jennifer and realized he was going to lose her if he continued arguing with the heartless personnel at the facility.

"Karuri, please let's go to the next hospital. Hope they will accept my card," he said desperately as he picked her up with the help of his brother.

The only thing they had done to her was to give her some first aid and some injections whose purpose he did not understand.

"You can't leave without paying for the services," they were stopped by a man in a white apron.

"Which services" Johnstone asked angrily.

Karuri removed two thousand shillings from his wallet and handed it to the cashier. He was given a receipt for the bill of one thousand eight hundred shillings and they left the hospital.

"Don't you have some money kept somewhere for such emergencies? I see that your wife is pregnant, what were you planning to do when she is due?" Karuri asked almost in contempt.

"You will never understand, my brother," he replied, a sad look on his face.

Chapter Two

As he walked towards the constituency office, he thought about all they went through on the day they took Jennifer to hospital. The days after and almost pleaded for mercy. Before, he never thought he was living in such a wretched place where no one cared for the other. His life had been smooth and he was happy to follow culture and traditions set by no one knows who. But all that had changed and he saw himself lose close friends within a very short time.

He went to three hospitals before he decided to go to the only hospital in town which would accept his card. He had avoided it because it lacked facilities. When he arrived there, they could not treat his wife, they referred her to their facility in the city. Even there, they had to refer her to another facility which had the equipment that she needed. However, they could not carry out some of the tests claiming that they were not covered in his package.

"What do we do now?" his brother asked.

"I don't know," he answered sadly in a resigned tone.

"We can't just sit here and do nothing. Haven't you saved anything for yourself?" his brother asked.

"You will never understand it brother no matter how much I try to explain it. I hardly receive any salary at the end of the month," he said shamefacedly.

His brother did not enquire further. He went to the receptionist to ask for more time.

"Excuse me, we would like to make a request for an extension of time since the tests required are not in the cover. We will need to look for the cash. Meanwhile, will anything be done for her?" he asked the lady behind the desk.

"We are sorry that the national scheme and his work scheme do not cover these important tests, we will monitor her and do what is possible within what the covers allow us to charge. Do not delay so much since these tests are very important. We cannot go ahead without them," the receptionist advised.

"We will do our best. Hope she and her child are not in danger?" he asked.

"They are okay for now but they are not out of danger. The baby might be in shock. We will be monitoring her progress. Please do your part hastily since we are tied and cannot do anything at the moment," the receptionist said.

"Thank you," he said as he and his brother walked out.

"You have heard what the lady has said," he said reflectively.

"I think we should try a fundraiser. I have no way of getting the money they require. By the way, do you have any that you can lend to me?" he asked hopefully.

"My brother, you know that my projects have not been doing well lately. If I had anything in my account, I would not allow Jennifer to suffer. What were you saying about a fundraiser? I think it would be a good idea," he said evading the line Kahiga was taking.

"I was just saying I cannot get that money myself. I did not mean it. It would take time to organize one and as you heard back there, we don't have the time," Kahiga said laughing.

"I am serious. You know with the current economy, the only thing we can do is organize a fundraiser. Perhaps people will respond," his brother said.

"I will try asking from my friends first," Kahiga said realizing his brother was not willing to help him with the money.

He asked for two days and realized no one was going to respond to him. He was not even asking to be given the money but rather borrowing it from them, but none wanted to hear about it. Eventually, he gave up and approached his brother to plan the fundraiser. His wife was deteriorating at the hospital and he had no one to turn to. All the schemes he had been contributing to had failed him at the hour of his need. Even the many groups he subscribed to could not help him. They only gave him what was written in their rule books, only enough to cater for his fare and nothing more.

He arrived at the constituency office at around nine in the morning. It was open but no one was in at that moment. He waited on the bench outside. One hour passed and still no one had arrived. The open door seemed to mock him. He was almost giving up two hours later when the MP's personal assistant arrived chatting loudly with a number of girls. They did not acknowledge him as they entered the office still chatting. They closed the door and stayed inside for another hour. He approached the door and knocked it, unable to take it anymore.

"Wait there or go home," the PA shouted from inside.

"What did we ever do to deserve this?" he asked himself as he went back to the bench.

The PA, the man inside with the girls, was a few years before his student. He dropped out of form three and joined the business world. When the political campaigns started, being an influential man in his circles, he aligned himself with the current member of parliament who made him his personal assistant. He behaved pompously with all those who had tried to advise him against abandoning school, though he was not doing well in his studies. Kahiga was one of those people who felt he needed to at least complete his studies to make it in life.

A few other people joined him on the bench. They all needed help from the man who a few years before had gone looking for them in their homes. At that moment, it was easier to see God face to face than that man. Like sugarcane that had been sucked of all its sweetness, they were fit for the bin as far as the man at the helm of the constituency and his handlers were concerned. They would become useful again during the next campaign periods.

"I always wonder if we came down here to push others to their destinies and forgot to go back where we belonged. Why do we have to always beg for services that we should rightfully receive?" a man seated next to Kahiga asked.

"Who told you it is your right? These are gods who must be worshipped if one wishes to live on the land. Woe unto you if you don't have the capacity to worship them. By the way, why are you here?" another man who sat at the edge of the bench asked.

"I am here for my daughter's bursary. This is the fifth time I am here and nothing has been forthcoming. The headteacher told me that she can go to work as a maid if I am not able to pay her fees," the first man said sadly.

"You should not get tired. I am also here for the same. And you, teacher Kahiga, don't tell me you are also here for the bursary?" the first man said facing Kahiga.

"Aren't you aware that his wife has been hospitalized?" the other man asked before Kahiga could even respond.

"Let me understand, if your wife is in hospital, are you here to be assisted with the hospital bill? Is your insurance cover not enough? If people like you come here to beg with us, where are we headed to?" the other man asked callously.

"You will never understand how this world operates. I think this country belongs to the very few up there, the rest of us have to worship them for us to survive…"

"Mr. Kahiga, you can come in now," a lady interrupted them before he could finish what he wanted to say.

Kahiga followed the lady inside. He had been there for more than four hours and it was not certain he was going to get the help he needed. This was the third time he was there for the same appointment and every time he would receive a different excuse why he could not be attended.

"Kate, do you know this man was my teacher?" the PA asked as he swung on the chair.

"Oh, I didn't know that. What does he want?" Kate asked as she sat on a chair facing Kahiga, revealing plump thighs which could hardly be covered by her short skirt.

Kahiga looked at the ceiling. He was wondering how long he was going to bear that embarrassment. The man in front of him was doing everything possible to humiliate him.

"Mr. Kahiga, even though you were always against me and did not believe in me, I can help you a lot. I am not a vindictive man," the PA said as he pulled some documents from the drawer.

"What is it that you wanted? Kate, please record everything in the book, honorable Kiriti will come back to the country next week. They went to Haiti on a benchmarking on effective health care and universal health cover," he added as he perused the documents.

The words sliced Kahiga like a sharp knife. He wanted to speak directly with the MP. It seemed that his wife would die before he even got a chance to meet him. It was strange how these men were unavailable when one needed them and always available when they needed you.

"I am here for the appointment I have with his honorable Kiriti. I was supposed to meet him today," Kahiga said looking at the man who could not hide his spite against him.

"You will have to tell me everything you wanted to tell him. I will inform him when he comes back if it is something worthy of his ears. By the way, did your wife get out of hospital?" the PA asked still perusing the documents in front of him.

"Not yet, in fact, I am here on that account," Kahiga responded.

"I am sorry about that. So, what can I do for you?" the PA asked indifferently.

"I wanted to talk to honorable Kiriti," Kahiga said almost in spite.

"You can't talk to him. I thought that you were an enlightened man," the PA said looking at the man spitefully.

"What do you mean by that?" Kahiga asked almost losing his patience.

If it were not for the fact that he needed to go through this man to get what he wanted, he would have already punched him. He had known him to be a very insolent man who never had any respect for his elders. He only bowed to those who had power, a bootlicker who only cared about what people could give him and how much power they yielded.

"Teacher, I think you should now leave the profession. I think it is getting you retarded. Are you not aware of protocol in government offices? No wonder you have remained in a desolate state despite many years of work. Look at your students, they have gone and excelled beyond measure while you remain a beggar among the people," the PA said thumping his chest.

Kahiga did not respond to that. He just looked at the ceiling wondering whether he would continue with the humiliation or look for help elsewhere.

"I know you are here to be helped with the hospital bills. Is the insurance not catering for it or you want some more money for your own pocket? I understand that you have the best health cover in the entirety of Africa, yet you were the people who were opposing the cover because it belonged to the member of parliament whom you are seeking help from," the PA continued to castigate him.

Kahiga almost wept. He remembered that his wife was at risk of losing her life and that of her unborn child because the insurance company had refused to approve some of the procedures that she needed. His heart felt heavy and he looked at his student and wondered if he really did not make a mistake to become a teacher.

"Why are you quiet? As I told you, you can only address your problems through me. You will never get to see him without my approval," the PA said pompously.

Kahiga was lost for words. Just as he was contemplating what to do, his phone rang. He excused himself and as he went out to pick the call, a tear dropped from his eyes.

Chapter Three

Nobody could tell exactly how it happened. He himself did not even get time to respond. Before their shouts reached the ears of the intended recipients, the man was flying in the air. The four by four SUV stopped about a hundred meters ahead with its bonnet dented. When he hit the ground, he was no more.

They gathered around him within seconds like flies on a carcass. The stunned woman driver was catatonic inside the car. She could not tell what had just happened. Even when rowdy men banged against her vehicle, she could not hear anything. They opened the door to her vehicle and pulled her outside. Before they could manhandle her, a police vehicle passing by the scene came to a halt and stopped them from their intended action.

"She must pay for this. They drive as if they are the only users of the road," one man shouted as one of the officers led the woman towards their vehicle to enquire from her what had just happened.

She was unresponsive. She was in a state of shock and therefore unable to recount anything. The police placed her in their car as they went to interrogate the bystanders who were the eyewitnesses to the accident.

"It was the man's fault, he was walking along the road without looking where he was going," a woman shouted from among the crowd.

"No, it was the lady. How could she drive so fast without considering the right of pedestrians to use the road?" a man in a bloodied white overall shouted back.

He was carrying a huge knife and his eyes were bloodshot. No one dared to contradict him. The police moved close to where he was and he started moving back as if he had something he was hiding from them.

"Please tell us what happened," one of the policemen requested ready to record everything on a notebook.

"I was not here. I have to go back to my work. Ask that woman, she owns that stall over there and she must have witnessed everything," the man said retreating to his shop.

"Coward," a man behind him mumbled but he did not hear it.

The police moved to the woman who owned the stall the man referred to and asked her what had happened. The woman stood upright and, like a reporter, started narrating what had happened according to her.

"The man seemed to be in deep thoughts. He was walking on the middle of the road. I think he was drunk, though he was not staggering. The driver of the vehicle, that woman," she pointed in the direction of the police car, "tried to avoid him but she could not. She hit him and he started flying like an angel. It happened so fast that no one could tell what had happened. We were all shocked to see the man landing and the car stopped just as he was hitting the ground."

"You are a liar. The man was walking on the pedestrian walk when the car came from nowhere and knocked him off," a man in a dirty apron with writings, Soin Insurance Company, countered.

The police could in the end not get a clear account of what exactly happened. Everyone had their own version of how the accident took place. They assessed the scene, wrote their report and after the man, who was then covered in a brown blanket had been taken away, they drove with the woman towards the station. Her car was towed to the station after them.

"You will have to record a statement with the police before we let you go, madam. Your car will remain in the station until after investigations have been completed," one of the officers told her when they arrived at the station.

She recorded the statement and called one of her friends to pick her from the station. She had had a very depressing day. The insurance company with which she had taken her child's education policy had gone under just when her policy was about to mature. Her daughter was studying in one of the most prestigious schools in the country and she had not yet paid her fees. Just when she received the news of the company going into receivership, she received the news that her daughter had been diagnosed with acute pneumonia and had been taken to one of the city hospitals. On reaching the hospital, she found out that the hospital had canceled all contracts with the company that she had taken her health scheme, the same company that had gone under receivership. She did not have any savings in her account and was at that moment paying a high mortgage that was taking a great toll on her finances. She was about to break up.

She was driving to her father's home in the village to find out if he could bail her out only for that foolish man to get on her way. She did not even know exactly what happened, she only found herself parking by the roadside after hitting someone. She was in shock and could not tell exactly what had transpired.

"Janet, what is going on? What happened and why are you in a police station?" her friend asked when she arrived.

"Please just take me home. I think my world is crumbling," Janet said breaking down.

Her friend allowed her to cry when they got into the car. She did not say a word to her for the thirty minutes she cried her heart out. When she had calmed down, she drove off from the station towards the city.

"You have a lot to explain to me," she said as she looked at her friend who seemed to be lost.

"Please take me to Living Health Hospital," Janet said flatly.

"What do you want there?" her friend asked shocked.

"Please take me there, Ashley," Janet said without explaining anything.

Janet was a short woman in her thirties working as a sales manager in one of the multinational companies in the country. She had a good salary and could afford most of the things young people desired. Her figure and chocolate complexion made her a social media influencer giving her a celeb status in the country. Because of this, she tried to live a life of her status as a celeb sinking her into many debts. She had met the father of her daughter in one of the national shows but he later dumped her after impregnating her. She had brought up the daughter all by herself vowing never to get into a relationship with any other man after her heartbreak. She continued her life as an influencer and appeared in the media for all the reasons the celebrities do.

Her father had been a permanent secretary in the first government and like many wise men, according to the language of the day, he had made considerable wealth from his position and its related connections. It was through those connections that he managed to get his daughter employed by the multinational company where she worked. It was rumored that he owned considerable shares in Soin Insurance Company, once owned by the government but then in the hands of a private company. It was said that during his tenure as permanent secretary, many companies dealing in finance and insurance went under leading to deaths of several individuals due to heart attacks and related complications.

"I am not driving you any further from here if you are not going to tell me what is going on," Ashley said parking the car by the roadside, about three kilometers from the hospital.

"It is okay. I am going to walk from here. Thanks for your help," Janet said attempting to open the door.

Ashley locked all the doors through the electrical system preventing her from getting out. She could see that her friend was going through a lot and the fact that she was in a police station was even going to add to her problems. Given her celebrity status, rumors would start doing rounds all over the country. She needed to know what was happening in order to counter what might ensue.

"Janet, you know your status in the country and what any scandal can do to you and your name. Please tell me what is going on. We should be able to get through it and protect your name," Ashley said concernedly.

"I don't care about any name or status. What have they gained me apart from depression and debts. I want my life for myself now," Janet said indifferently.

"What is going on?"

Ashley realized that whatever her friend was going through was beyond what she could imagine. All her life, she had lived to protect her name. She had to do so many crazy things to maintain her status. To hear her talk like that was inconceivable.

"Please take me to the hospital. I need to be there urgently. And please, when we get there, will you please help me in contacting my father. I was going to see him when it all happened. Tell him to get to me as soon as he can," Janet said, her tone that of someone who had nothing more to do with life.

"Why don't I call him now?" Ashley asked.

"No, I need to know how my daughter is first," Janet said without explaining.

"What about your daughter?"

Ashley was getting more perplexed by the moment. She looked at her friend and then back to the road. She realized that if she did not concentrate, she would cause an accident. She had not even got the chance to ask her friend where she had taken her car. She did not get the chance to see it at the police station. She cared a lot about her friend and realizing that she was going through a lot at that moment gave her so much stress.

When they arrived at the hospital, she followed her friend without asking any questions. She realized that her friend needed space and she was not going to be unjust towards her. She still had not discovered what she wanted to do at the hospital and what had happened to her daughter. It was as if she had become a stranger to her best friend.

"Please go and call my father as I talk to the nurses," Janet said when they arrived on the fourth floor of Sion Hospital where the pediatric wards were located.

Ashley did not want to imagine that her friend's daughter could be hospitalized and yet she had not got to know about it. She did not ask any questions but hoped she was there on another matter and not on account of her daughter. She did not even know what to tell her father when she called him. She knew him as a stubborn old man who never listened to anyone and never accepted any counsel from anyone apart from his own. Getting him to leave his office to respond to her daughter's call was going to be an elephant task.

She searched her phonebook and when she located his number, she moved to the elevator. She waited for it to get to the ground floor and when the doors opened, she changed her mind and moved to the end of the corridor where there were no people. She dialed the number and waited for the man to pick up.

"Hello, this is Ashley, Janet's friend," she said.

"No, no, it is not like that. I am not asking for anything from you. I am not asking any money from you," she said in response to the voice from the other end.

"Janet needs you at Sion Hospital," she said and hung up before the man could ask any questions.

She went back to the reception and found her friend had already left. What was happening to her? Why was she treating her that way? She had not done anything to her to warrant such treatment. The only thing she had done was to help her. Why was she being so cold towards her?

"Excuse me, do you happen to know where the lady we came with is?" she asked the receptionist.

The receptionist looked at her like she was lost and almost insulted her. There had been so many people at her desk that day and she would have had to be a superhuman to be able to recall everyone who passed through her.

"So many people have passed through here and I may not be able to recall them all. Unless you give me more details, I may not be able to help you," the receptionist said politely.

"Oh, sorry, her name is Janet. I am her friend Ashley," she said confused.

"Oh, Ashley. Would you happen to know what your friend came to do here? There are several people by the name Janet. This is a pediatric ward and most of them have come to visit their children. Would you happen to know which child she came to visit?" the receptionist asked.

Ashley was not certain how to answer that question. She still hoped that Janet was not there for her daughter but rather for something else.

"I am not so sure. Her daughter's name is Daisy, Daisy Nkatha. She was well and I believe she is at school now. She told me to bring her here but she did not tell me why. I am afraid something could be happening to her and she is not willing to talk about it," Janet said.

"Oh, the short pretty lady? She said you wait for her here. She will be back in a while," the receptionist said pointing to the waiting bay a few meters from her desk.

Ashley had no choice but to go and wait for her friend as she had been instructed. She was worried about her but there was nothing she could do about it.

Chapter Four

Kahiga did not return to the PA's office after the call. He was like one who was demented when he received the call. He ran like a mad man and picked the first means of transport he could find along the way. He felt that life had been sent to punish him. He could not understand why everything had to happen to him at the same time just when he thought he was beginning to enjoy his own life. He had plans of building his family a nice home and was in the process of topping up a loan with his savings and credit society when hell broke loose.

He had thought it was good news that his wife was expecting another child just at the moment they had started living happily as a family since they tied the knot several years before. When he approached his SACCO, he was shocked to learn that apart from not being able to offer him the loan he was looking for, all his savings were about to sink with it. Some officials had embezzled the society's funds by awarding themselves and their cronies' huge loans and got it under receivership. That was the beginning of his depression.

When he arrived home and explained everything to his wife, she was very positive about everything. She was not disappointed as he had expected but rather encouraged him to take everything calmly.

"Do not worry my dear. What we cannot control we leave to God, He knows everything. You will get back your money sooner or later," she had told him when he narrated everything that had happened at the society's offices.

"But that is very unfair. One has worked so hard to save in order to be able to do something and then they take away everything. I wish I had known, I would not have saved a coin with the SACCO," he said lamenting.

"Do not regret my dear. Everything happens for a reason and those who have stolen from the members will pay for their sins," she continued encouraging him.

He was looking so stressed and at the verge of giving up. She looked at him and wondered if he was the same man who never gave her any peace at home. He was a human being after all and expected so much from others more than he himself could do. Listening to him, one would have thought he would never bow to any challenge in life. She remembered the many times he had reprimanded her for not being able to do things he expected her to do though without explaining how.

"There is something I want to tell you," she said after a brief moment of silence.

"I don't know what they want with us. They increased the deduction for the national health fund, then they removed the medical allowance in favor of a policy we do not understand. How do they expect us to survive with nothing left on our pay slips while we are servicing huge loans with interest rates that are increasing daily?" he asked as if he had not heard what she had said.

"Don't think too much. Everything is going to work out. You will see," she said caressing his chest.

"What is it that you wanted to tell me?" he asked.

She had thought he had not heard her. She was wondering how he was going to react when she told him the news. He had been a man who wanted many children. Even before he married her, he had told her that he wanted at least six children in his house. She had thought he was joking but it appeared that he was really serious about it.

"Children are a blessing and it is important to have as many as possible. You never know which one among them would do well in life," he had told her to her dismay.

"One can only thank God for the ones He gives them. They are a gift from God and we cannot demand more than He can give. We can only go by his will," she had told him.

"Some things are not about faith or such things that people call faith. God released them to us and we are free to make our choices. We cannot blame

God for our failures. If a woman cannot give birth to as many children as are necessary, I have no business with that woman," he retorted and she realized he was serious.

She would not disappoint him. If that was what he wanted, she had no intention to contradict him.

"You wanted to tell me something. Why are you quiet then?" he asked facing her.

"I am going to give you another child," she said in a soft tone.

"That is really wonderful. That calls for celebration. I wish it was daytime. I would have gone out with my friends to celebrate the good news," he said as he left the bed for the living room.

His wife was shocked. She did not know what he wanted to do. He had been one to take one or two bottles, though he never got violent because of it. He would not be crazy enough to go looking for his friends just because she had given him such news.

Before she could come up with a logical answer, he returned to the bedroom with a bottle of scotch.

"I always keep one in the cupboard to make me merry for such moments. You are not going to take it though, it is not good for the child," he said as he poured himself a glass.

Such memories made him feel sad as the van drove towards town. He wondered what the hospital wanted to say to him. They had said it was urgent. He could only think of the worst, though he hoped everything was well. He still had not got the money to pay for the procedures his wife needed. If that was why they called him, they would have to wait for a little bit longer. The people and the sources he relied on had all hit a rock, but he was not giving up yet.

Then there were the health schemes he subscribed to and paid high premiums for that he had no control of. He often heard stories of misdiagnoses and medical negligence, but he had not been aware they were of such grave magnitude until he took his wife to the hospital. He remembered the story of his colleague who had had a wrong tooth extracted.

"I wish we were allowed to select our own insurance scheme at least. The facilities they recommend are all run by quacks," Mr. Daminti had told him one evening as they went home.

"Why do you say so? I think it is better this way because if they gave us the money, we would not have the discipline to take a health scheme. In fact, I would have engaged mine in a bigger loan," Kahiga said.

"You do not know what you are talking about. Before, we could choose our own doctors, nowadays, even if they gave you a cleaner, you can't complain. Else, you can choose to forego the facilities they recommend and pay from your own pocket which would be really unfair given we are paying very high premiums for it. I know of people who are receiving ten times better services than we do yet they pay lesser premiums than we do," Mr. Daminti lamented.

"So, what happened to you?" Kahiga asked, unwilling to listen to more lamentations.

He felt that the citizens had become so disillusioned and complained about everything, even things that were meant to help them. They seemed not to understand that nothing worked perfectly, not even in those nations they highly praised. Instead of finding ways of making their nation better and assisting their leaders to achieve development goals, all they did was to complain.

"I went to a clinic with a tooth ache on my right side. I spent over four hours on the queue, I had gone there at four in the morning and the hospital opened doors at nine in the morning to serve us. So, you can imagine I am counting the hours from nine not four when I got there and found multitudes waiting for services. When I went to the consultation room, I spent only two minutes and was sent to the dentist with a prescription. After two hours of pain, I don't think they used anesthesia on me, I found out they had removed my only functional tooth, if you know what I mean. I cannot chew hard food now. I am relying on mashed potatoes and other soft food," Mr. Daminti said angrily.

"Then you should sue them," Kahiga said indifferently.

He still felt that the man was exaggerating and lacked patriotism. These were the people who always talked ill of their country and always wanted to go seek for greener pastures abroad instead of watering the grass in their pastures.

He understood everything when his wife was taken ill. Several days had passed and he still did not have any idea what to do. For the first time, he started to feel like he was not a citizen of the country he was so proud of. He realized that those who were complaining never lacked patriotism; they suffered in a land that was supposed to protect them and they did not know who to turn to.

He arrived at the hospital at four in the evening; tired, hungry and dejected. He had no time to think about all those things. All he wanted was to know why they had called him there. He was already feeling guilty that he could not stay with his wife at the hospital, or rather, he could not visit her as much as he wanted. Even though he did, she could not communicate with her. Her life and that of the child she was carrying were in danger and he needed to move with haste. His efforts were being made futile by forces he could not control. He was feeling helpless and for the first time in his life, he doubted his abilities as a man.

"Hello, I am here," he said hastily to the lady at the reception.

He literally did not know what to tell her. He felt ashamed as a man that he could not provide for his own family. He could not give them the most basic things. Back at home, his children were wondering what was going on. He had not got the chance to explain to them what was happening. They were feeling like they had been abandoned by their parents. He never got time to interact with them. He left home early in the morning and would go back late in the night full of thoughts about how he was going to solve the situation before him.

"Who are you and how can I help you?" the lady at the reception asked.

She was a different one from the one he usually found. She was therefore not aware of his situation. She could tell that he was a man in desolation and wondered what he wanted.

"I am Johnstone Kahiga. My wife is in the intensive care unit. I brought her here several days ago and…" he could not continue.

The weight bore heavily on him and he moved a few steps backwards, sat on the bench and held his head between his legs.

"I don't know what to do," he cried out.

"Please calm down," the lady at the reception said.

She gave him a cup of coffee and after he had taken it, she directed him to a room at the further end of the block.

"Please go to room seventeen. You will get help there," she said sympathizing with him.

He walked slowly as she watched him. He seemed to be carrying the entire world on his shoulders. He looked haggard and the trousers were falling from him. He had lost much weight and it appeared if he continued that way, he would be replacing his wife at the hospital.

"Please take a seat," the man behind the desk told him when he entered the room.

"Thank you," he said, falling on the chair like a bundle of firewood.

"Can I have some water please," he said after he had sat.

"Charity, please bring some water here and also find out if there is some food left in the kitchen," the man shouted.

"You need to be strong for your children. You cannot solve all the problems there are in the world. Take everything calmly and do just what you can. There are many people relying on you," the man said.

"I know, doctor, but I think this nation has reduced us into wretched wrecks who cannot do anything for anyone. We are only fit for the graves and I think the only thing we wait and hope for is the grave. They have taken away everything from us," Kahiga said in a dejected tone.

"You cannot talk like that. There is so much you can do and you are such a strong man. Do not allow the challenges of life to cloud your thinking. You need to be more positive about life," the man said.

He was a young man, probably in his early thirties. He was wearing a white overall coat and seemed like he had just been employed. He looked at the man before him, he did not look old. He was probably in his late forties but his appearance made him look like he had been taken from the stone age. By the look of things, he seemed like he had been a strong man before the calamities struck him.

"What is there to be positive about? We give out so much from our labor and toil to secure our deaths. It seems that it is the only thing that we work hard for, and are hoping for. No one will give you a hand until you are dead. Even the health insurance we take seem to be more concerned about the last respects, as they call it. So, all our efforts are to secure a decent death, if there is anything like that," he said optimistically.

"You are a funny and philosophical man. But there is more to life than what you think, if you open your eyes and focus hard enough," the young man said.

"You don't know what you are saying, young man. When you get enlightened, you will realize that the only thing we are working for is death. It seems it is the only thing people in this country celebrate," Kahiga said in a melancholic tone.

"What did you call me here for?" he asked not wishing to take the argument further.

Chapter Five

The children woke up at a quarter to nine. They wanted to make the most of their time before schools opened to catch up on sleep. Their father had already gone. They could not understand why he was leaving them alone and neither why they had not seen their mother for several days. They wondered if she had left them.

"Where did mother go?" the youngest child, a boy aged seven asked.

The oldest of the three, a boy of eleven years looked at him and did not know what to say. He was wondering what was going on at home. They never found their father in the house when they woke up and their mother had gone missing for more than three days. When their father returned home in the evening, he always looked so tired that they could not ask him anything. He would get busy cooking them supper and preparing them to go to bed. Though he did not reprimand them as before, he looked sad and instructed them calmly. He never gave them a chance to ask any question. Whenever they tried to, he told them that he needed rest and he certainly looked like he needed it badly.

"I don't know what is going on but I heard that mother is in hospital," the eldest child said.

His name was Karangi. He looked taller for his age and the absence of his parents made him behave more maturely than he would have naturally. He took care of the others when his father was away. The second one, a girl of eight years had stopped going out to play with the other children. She drooped outside her mother's bedroom most of the time. She was missing her very much.

"Why can't we go to visit her? We should not just wait for her here. I will ask father to take us to her when he comes home this evening," the girl said beginning to brighten up.

"Please take your tea and we will see what we can do. We should help father with some of the household chores now that he is going through so much. We will wash the utensils and sweep the compound instead of watching TV all day," the eldest child said.

"Hooray, we are going to help father," the girl said looking for a broom to start sweeping the compound.

"Please take your tea first then we can do the rest later," Karangi told her sister.

"Do we have bread today?" she asked.

The youngest boy was already taking a second cup. He did not care about bread. The girl could not take tea without bread.

"No, I think father forgot once again," Karangi said.

"Then I am not taking tea. Let me start sweeping, you will join me when you are through," the girl said moving outside.

"But he left some money for us. I think he wants us to buy bread," Karangi said taking the one hundred shillings note that had been placed under the thermos.

"Did he leave anything for lunch?" the girl asked.

"No, I don't see anything else apart from the tea and the money," Karangi said.

"Then we should use the money to buy lunch. Please hurry up and let us finish the work fast. Maybe father will come early today and he will take us to see mother when he comes," the girl said hopefully.

The boys took their tea and joined the girl outside. The home looked deserted. Though the morning sun shone brightly, a frightening atmosphere engulfed the compound and they felt as if they were in the dark facing ferocious ghosts that tried to harm them.

"I feel scared," the youngest boy said.

"You should not be scared, Kanini," Karangi told him.

"I am also worried, Karangi. Let us go back to the house," the girl said as she dropped the broom.

"What are you scared of, Kelly? We should complete the cleaning first and then go back to the house," Karangi said.

"I don't think we are safe outside. I think we should go to grandmother's house. It is not far," Kanini said pulling his brother.

"Father told us not to leave the house," Karangi told them.

"But I am scared," Kelly said beginning to cry.

"We have been here alone for three days and nothing has happened to us. You should not worry about anything," Karangi tried to convince them though he too was feeling the same scare hanging over the compound, as if it was trying to warn them to run away.

He was trying to be brave and did not want to show his siblings that he was scared. The atmosphere was unusual that day. It was as if death was lurking in their home. They had never felt that scared even when their parents had left them alone and arrived late in the night. There were times they even stayed in the house an entire night yet they did not feel scared as they were that day.

Just as they were contemplating what to do to escape the scary presence, someone called from the gate. They were somehow relieved only for Kelly to scare them again by reminding them about a movie they had watched in which a witch stole children by taking the form of a neighbor. They ran back to the house locking themselves inside.

"Karangi, are you in. Where is your father?" a woman called from outside.

"He went out but has not come back," Karangi answered from inside the house.

"And why are you hiding yourselves in the house?" the woman asked.

She was a friend to their mother. She had gone looking for their father to establish how her friend was fairing and also to tell him that his mother wanted to see him. They had not seen him since the calamity that befell the family that morning. It was not like him to act with such negligence.

The children went out of the house looking scared. They looked at the woman still wondering whether she was real or she was the witch they had seen on TV.

"Why do you look so scared?" the woman asked as she approached them.

"Where is your father? Did he go to the hospital?"

The children answered by shaking their heads. They did not understand anything about what was going on.

"Please lock the house and let us go to your grandmother's house," the woman told them.

The children reluctantly locked the house and followed the woman to their grandmother's house. Several people had gathered at the home and some young men were erecting a tent in the compound.

"Please serve them some food," their grandmother instructed the woman.

After she had served the children, the woman went to talk with the old woman.

"He is not yet back. I wonder why he has taken so long to inform us about what happened at the MP's office. I am also wondering if he has not learnt anything about his brother," the woman said as she sat next to Karangi's grandmother.

"I don't know what is happening in my family. It is as if the devil has put up tent here to destroy it," the woman lamented.

"Should I call Kahiga?" the woman asked.

"His phone is off. Let us wait for him," the old lady said.

As they talked, a black car drove into the compound. A man in a black suit alighted and approached them.

"Are you Karuri's mother?" the man asked after greeting them.

"Yes. What do you want?" the old lady asked.

"Can I talk with you in private?" the man asked.

"What is it you have to tell me that you cannot say in front of all these people?" the woman asked pointing at the people gathered in her compound.

"It is an important issue about your son," the man said calmly.

"Please go to the house with him," the woman who was chatting with her advised.

The man and the old lady went into the house.

"Can the children stay?" the old lady asked as she ushered him into the living room.

"Was he their father?" the man asked.

"No, their uncle," she replied.

"I would prefer if they did not hear what we are talking about, though it is not something wrong," the man said.

"Karangi, please take your food and eat from outside. If your father comes, tell him to come inside," she instructed the children.

"What is it that you wanted to say? I hope you are not one of those con artists who prey on ignorant people. I will call the police on you if I suspect anything of the sort. We are tired of being conned," the old lady said as she called outside for the man to be served.

"Nyakio, please serve him some tea."

They were both silent as they waited for tea to be served. The man was looking at the portraits on the walls which indicated that the family was an affluent one, or at least during their days, they were. It represented a lifestyle typical of the eighties civil servants who owned large cash crop plantations. The walls were painted plain blue. The paint seemed to have faded a little but it was good by any standards.

The portrait of the man with a cap indicated the man was once a police officer. There were several portraits showing him receiving awards from the head of state. The stars on his shoulders showed that he was not an ordinary ranking officer. That explained why he could afford to build his family such a house, though not stylish by the contemporary standards, it stood out among the rest and had been a point of reference for many years. It was a five-bedroomed house built in a simple English style.

"Where is his father now? He looks like a famous man though I have not got the chance to meet him," he asked pointing at Karuri's father's photo.

"Oh, Karangi? He was such a nice man. He died in the line of duty. Just when he had got his promotion as inspector. He never got to watch his children grow. I have brought them up in great poverty and many challenges since no one was willing to help me. They thought we had a lot of money and could not believe that sometimes we went without food. I never allowed my sons to miss anything though and they grew to be respectable men. Oh, the cruel hand of death," she said sadly holding her head in her two hands.

"What happened to his benefits? They should have been enough to take care of the family needs given his rank," the man said in an expectant tone.

He had come to the house with the hope of securing one case, seems his mother's prayers were working miracles. He would get yet another task. Though he did not believe in his mother's God, and all the things associated with religion, at least her faith seemed to work mysteries that he could not deny. He never believed in luck, but it seemed he was luck itself. He never cared about anyone, all he cared about was money and many of his clients were lamenting as he grew in wealth and power. He was even thinking of taking a political position.

"We have been following it up for the last fifteen years. All they do is give us excuses, sending us to different offices and demanding several other things. I am already giving up on it," the woman said looking at the man who had been her companion in her youth.

"Don't worry about it anymore. I will make sure you get your money the fastest possible. I am advocate Lennington of Lennington and Sons Inc," he said handing her a card.

Just at that moment, Nyakio entered with a kettle of tea and two metal cups. She served them with what could be called black tea. It seemed the cows were on protest and produced white water instead of milk.

"Do you need anything else?" she asked looking at the old lady.

"No, just make sure the children are taken care of. Has Kahiga arrived? I need him here urgently," the old lady asked as she took her cup of tea. Lennington never touched his.

"Not yet. We are still trying to contact him but none of his numbers is going through," Nyakio said.

Chapter Six

J anet could not come to terms with what the doctor had told her. She tried to imagine what she could have done to face all that misfortune but no logic surfaced. Though she had become famous in the social circles, though she did not know the exact reason for her fame, she never treated anyone meanly. She did her work perfectly and helped those who needed her help. In fact, she felt that if all the people she had helped could be gathered together, she would deserve a Nobel prize for her acts of philanthropy. Maybe that was what made her popular. But was life repaying her goodness with calamities? Was the case about family altars true? But then, why did it reward some and punished others, especially those who tried to be good to others?

She could not deny her father was a wicked man. Though he had helped her a lot in her career progression and giving her a decent living, he had made many families cry. He seemed to be living his life on the greener side. He had no worries about anything and everything he did succeeded, just like his father before him. Most of her charity works were somehow in a way to atone for her father's sins. But why was she suffering for trying to correct what was wrong?

"My daughter, no one ever succeeded in this world by being good. Take advantage of every opportunity you get. Let people cry and worship you on your way to success, you will even get more powerful and they will surrender their wealth to you. But if you continue showing them kindness, not only will you lose your wealth, you will lose your control and power over them. Eventually no one will remember you. Steal whatever is on your way that is of value, kill whatever obstructs your way. By any means crush and conquer. That is what the world is all about. Whatever you do is to make you more powerful and make people fear and let no one deceive you," her father had told her when she shared her intention to start a foundation to help the less privileged in the society.

"But father, that is wicked. We need to lift people as we rise. That is the only way to attract blessings and there is dignity in uplifting the lives of the people," Janet countered.

"You talk like a foolish girl. You are the wicked one, foolish and untrained in the ways of the world. Do you think I would be where I am by being good to people? Whatever you seek to do, even those called acts of kindness, make sure it is to make you more powerful and feared among the people. If anything, the only people you can help are the dead. They cannot take anything from you and they cannot compete with you. When you get there, give them the kindness you are talking about, maybe they will remember you wherever they are going and help your ways. The insurance to your wealth and power is to make people invest in you and when they have given you every coin, and they cannot live anymore, you wipe the tears of their relatives by a small token to make more invest in you. Let them secure their death by making you great and powerful," the man advised.

"You speak like the devil. I wonder whether you are even my father. I cannot subscribe to your gospel, not now, not ever," Janet said angrily.

"Then you cannot be my daughter as well. To me everything is an investment, you too are an investment and I always look for value of return for all my investments. Go and be valuable and I promise, you will be your father's daughter and I will make you great," the man said.

Janet stormed out of the house and banged the door against him. He was unbothered. He knew she would go looking for him sooner or later. Janet never looked back. She gathered her friends and raised funds and established the foundation to lift young girls from the shackles of poverty by teaching them valuable life skills. That is how she gained celebrity status and organizations came to her aid in her quest to make life tolerable for the underprivileged.

She never thought she would go looking for her father ever again. She wanted to prove him wrong by succeeding and making many succeed through kindness. That is until everything she held onto started crumbling. First, the company she was working for went bankrupt under unexplainable circumstances, then the insurance company she had invested most of her savings also went under. Everything about her world was working as if to prove her father right. She had no choice but to go looking for him to aid her recover her footing. Even though she did not intend to compromise her stand, she would play the fool and reestablish herself. Most of the organizations, and friends who supported her before had deserted her at that crucial moment.

Then her daughter had been taken ill. She had no money for her treatment. And then that foolish man appeared from nowhere when she went looking for her father. What was happening? Were the systems designed to punish all good efforts? It was ironical that at the time her calamities were piling up on her, her father's net worth was hitting the roofs. Media reports indicated that he was joining the league of the wealthiest individuals in the continent.

"My daughter, you need to get up from that bed. We cannot let them win," Janet pleaded with the unconscious girl.

"Who cannot be allowed to win?" Ashley asked from the door.

Janet was startled. She had not expected anyone to be with her in the room. She had no idea of how long she had been in the ward. She had even forgotten about her friend. She released her daughter's hand and embraced her friend and started crying.

"The wicked will always be in control and there seems to be nothing we can do," she said amidst sobs.

When Ashley realized her friend would not be getting to her any moment soon, she decided to ask the receptionist's help to track her friend. She had no idea what she was doing at the hospital. She thought that she had started helping the sick as well through her organization. Nothing could have warned her that her daughter was in that hospital. She had kept quiet about it all through. No wonder she was behaving strangely.

"When did she come here? Why did you not inform me about it," she asked caressing her friend who was still crying, mumbling unintelligible things.

"We cannot allow them to win, Ashley. We have to do something. We cannot allow the wicked to continue oppressing the people and causing them suffering," Janet said.

"We will talk about that later. What happened to your daughter?" she asked leading Janet to the only chair in the ward.

"Tell me what is happening?" Ashley asked shocked by the turn of events.

"Daisy was taken ill at the school. She was brought here but they are saying they cannot treat her since the institution has cancelled all contracts with the insurance company where I had taken my health policy. I don't have the money to pay for her treatment. All my savings sank with the insurance company where I had made my investments. Then when I was going home this morning I knocked down a man. I think he died, I have not heard any information about him since. That is why I called you to pick me at the station after I recorded my statement. I…" she started crying uncontrollably.

"You have to leave now," a nurse said at the door.

"How do you expect her to leave her daughter? Don't you have a heart?" Ashley asked angrily.

"It is the hospital policy," the nurse said politely.

"What kind of a foolish policy is that that denies a mother time with her child?" Ashley was almost blowing off.

"It is okay, Ashley. We need to go. I have to figure out how I am going to get money for treatment," Janet said kissing her daughter on the forehead.

"I will be back to see you soon. Please get up from that bed. We have a lot to do and we cannot allow them to win," she said and they left the room to the sound of the machines monitoring her daughter.

When they were outside, Ashley looked at her friend and felt really bad for her. She had no idea that she was going through so much. That made her even wonder what true friendship was all about. If she could not even tell her what she was going through, what was she there for? And there she was blaming her for neglecting her. There and then, she determined to be a good friend. She would check on her every moment and help with everything she could. The first thing she would do was to find a way of assisting her with the treatment of her daughter. She knew she required a lot of money. That hospital was attended by the most important people in the society and hospital bills were beyond most families reach. Only politicians and wealthy businessmen could afford treatment there.

Even before Janet's daughter received any treatment, her hospital bill had accumulated to half a million shillings. She was barely a day in the facility.

"Did you call the old man?" Janet interrupted her thoughts.

"Yes, I did. What is going on between you two?" Ashley asked concerned.

"Why do you ask?" Janet asked disinterestedly.

"When I called him, he asked me if you had changed your mind. Even when I told him you are at the hospital, he did not care to know what you are doing here," Ashley said a worried look on her face.

The old man did not even care to know whether his daughter had got into an emergency. He just told Ashley if Janet had changed her mind to go and see him to make things right before Ashley hung up in anxiety.

"Just leave the old man alone. I think he is part of the problems we need to deal with. The reason many people are suffering," Janet said without explaining.

"I think you have a lot to tell me. When are you planning to tell it all to me?" Ashley asked seriously.

"Don't worry. You are going to learn about it all soon," Janet said.

"What are you going to do about Daisy's treatment?" Ashley asked without pestering further.

"I am still trying to figure it out. She needs some procedures to be carried out but they are very expensive. She might not make it if I do not get the money on time," she said sadly.

"We have to do something, there must be something we can do and we must figure it out," Ashley said thinking deeply.

"We will get a way. I intend to go see the old man tomorrow. Maybe he will be humane enough to consider the plight of his granddaughter," Janet said drearily.

"I have an idea and I know it is going to work," Ashley beamed as she stopped her friend at the parking place to explain her brilliant idea.

"What is it?" Janet asked looking keenly at her friend who seemed to be out of her mind.

"You are a celebrity," she exclaimed.

"So, what does that have to do with your idea?" Janet asked beginning to lose interest.

"It is time all the people that know you came to your aid and gave back for what you have done for them," Ashley said expectantly.

"You are crazy. You will not turn me into a beggar. No, not when I can work with my hands. I will figure out what to do. You don't need to worry. Can we go home now?" Janet said pointing at the car.

"I was just trying to help. You don't have to be so mean to me," Ashley said disappointed.

Chapter Seven

"It seems you are right on that point. I have been trying to understand the systems and I am coming to realize that what you are saying is true. Life doesn't matter to many people. What matters is what they are going to make from you. Profit matters more than anything else, and to the people, everything is business. Even health has been turned into a profit minting venture," the doctor said sadly.

"We don't have to keep on talking about that now. It will not change anything and it is not going to help us," Kahiga said.

"Maybe there is something we can do. We are the ones who give these people the power. Without us, they can do nothing, but they have made it to appear as if we cannot do without them. What if we showed them the fact that they need us and not the other way round?" the young doctor said reflectively.

Kahiga was beginning to get impatient. But the young man was saying something important and worth considering, but how was anyone going to go about doing that. As it were, it is very hard to convince people to support a cause, even that which is meant to help them.

"And how do you think this is going to be achieved? They have the money and the power. They will always use these against us," Kahiga said countering.

"There is always a way if one is determined," the young man said.

"Now, tell me why you called me here. I guess we have to deal with the most urgent things first before we can think about the impossibilities. My wife is here, I don't even know whether she is going to get out alive. So, let us stop discussing them and deal with what concerns us," Kahiga said resignedly.

"Everything concerns us. In fact, what we are saying is the most urgent thing to deal with. If not for the greed for profits, we would not be in the situation we are in now. People would not die like flies just because someone is looking to make more money from the problems of the people," the young doctor said in a serious tone.

He looked at the man before him and saw the perfect moment to break the news. He knew he would be devastated, but that is what everybody went through because of the system. The schemes were made to deliberately not work so people can make money from them. The idea behind them was great but the executors were animals who sought to gnaw the flesh of every soul that intended to use them.

"What situation are you talking about? If you are referring to the country, I think a time has come for every individual to carry their own cross. I have to think about how to get my wife treated before I can think of how to change the country and stop greedy individuals from making profits of the weak citizens," Kahiga said in an almost callous tone.

He was thinking to himself that fleecing people seemed to be the only sure way of making it rich in the land. One had to think of how to get money from the people by any means. It did not matter whether that way was going to kill them, provided money flowed into one's account. Thinking about others and caring for their plight seemed to be the surest way of digging a hole for yourself into poverty. Everything was designed to fleece the people and those who excelled in the trade continued to get richer.

"I think everything is connected. Think about your wife for instance, she was a victim of the system that is designed to swindle the people. It is a system that doesn't care at all about what people are going through and what they are going to lose. Whether people die or not is none of their business. All they care about is money. How much profit they are going to make. They will remove money from your pocket by any means and using ways you can never understand. They will only console you with a little amount when you or your loved one loses their life. Even then, they are still making profit from you but they would make you believe that they are helping you," the young man said.

"And why is my wife a victim?" Kahiga asked alarmed.

He had not thought this man was going to bring his wife into the discussion. All the time, he thought he wanted to discuss about her treatment. He did not understand what he meant by victim.

"Your wife was expecting a child. She should have been attended the first moment she arrived here and the hospital should have looked for ways of recovering its bills after they had done their work. They should not have waited for you to raise the money before they began the treatment. They knew it was not your fault that your health scheme was not working. I know you people are paying a lot of money as premiums to the companies, though it is not clear how much since it is not disclosed in the systems. It was better when everyone received their medical allowance, they would choose the cover to take. She was such a young woman, expecting a child and I believe raising other children. Did she have to lose her life while so young," the young man dropped the bombshell.

Kahiga seemed like one hit on the face with ice cold water. His jaw dropped and he looked at the man before him as if he were an apparition. He did not hear another word the man said. When he had got some strength, he stood and approached the man slowly and quietly. The man seemed to be mumbling something, but Kahiga could not hear anything. The only sound in his mind was:

"Did she have to lose her life while so young?"

He held the man by the collar of his shirt, lifted him from the chair he sat on and growled at him.

"Can you repeat everything you have just told me."

"I am so sorry. She was such a lovely woman," the young doctor said.

"Are you out of your mind? You are going to give me back my wife," Kahiga shouted attracting the attention of the people outside the room.

"Please calm down. We did everything we could but she lost the battle," the doctor tried to explain.

"Everything you could? Are you kidding me?" Kahiga asked angrily.

He had begun choking the man. If no one appeared at that moment to help him, he would kill him adding to his troubles. He was not aware what he was doing. All that was running in his mind was how much he had struggled to get the money for her treatment, and even before he could get it, they had killed her. They were all going to pay for it. All of them would pay for Jennifer's life. She was not supposed to die.

"You are going to kill me. Please…" the words could not come of the doctor's mouth as Kahiga tightened his hold.

The young doctor started sweating and tried to reach the bell on his desk. It was a bit far. Kahiga did not realize it, and if he did, he did not care. The doctor used all the energy he had and rescued himself from the man momentarily and pressed the bell.

Kahiga was not done with him. He grabbed him again and this time held him by the neck. He applied pressure on it and the man started grunting.

"You are all the same. Did you think I was going to forgive you just because you gave me all that trash? What were you doing when she died? Why did you not try to save her life?" he was shouting angrily.

He moved the man to the wall and lifted him to the window ledge. He looked outside and lamented.

"No, this is too low for you. You are going to join her shortly," he said spittle flowing from his mouth.

"Please calm down and leave him. We are going to sort everything out," a nurse told him from the door.

"Stay where you are or he is going to die. You will not blame me for that," Kahiga warned.

"Please let him go and explain to us what happened. I know there is something we can do about it," the nurse said as he moved away a bit.

Kahiga grabbed a syringe from the table as he momentarily released the man who had now grown so weak to stand. Before he could drop to the ground, Kahiga grabbed him and pointed the syringe on his neck.

"Get out of my way," he warned the people who had gathered at the door.

He moved the man out of the room into the corridor. He entered with him into the elevator and pressed the button to floor number five. No one dared to follow them, fearing he was going to fulfill his threat. However, some men hurriedly took the next elevator and warned those in the other floors to wait at the exit. They hoped he would not harm the man while on the elevator.

Inside the elevator, Kahiga still held the man while pointing the syringe on his throat. He did not care what they were going to do to him. They had killed his wife and he was going to kill them all. All those damned systems were going to answer for what they had done to her.

"Why are you people so wicked. Does money matter to you more than people's lives. How many times did I beg you to treat her? How many phone calls did I make? Do you know how many offices I have visited? Do you even know what my children are going through? Are we paying to secure our death in this country?" he asked furiously.

At the fifth floor, Kahiga dragged the man from the elevator still threatening the men who were waiting at the exit. He was not going to let any one of them escape. When he was done with the man, he would turn to the others. They would all pay for their sins.

"Climb on the ledge," he warned the man.

When the man hesitated, he lifted him with all the strength he had and placed him on the window ledge. The window did not have a grill, which was perfect for him. He looked down and noted that the ground was far enough for him to accomplish his mission.

"Jump now," he ordered.

"Please stop it," the people surrounding him shouted.

He did not listen to them. They had not listened to him when he cried out to them to treat his wife, why should he listen to them.

"If you are not going to jump, I am going to push you myself and if need be we are going down together. I know they will be after me. I only hope that they will be kind enough to take care of my children," he lamented as he tried to climb on the ledge while still holding on to the man.

Before his foot stepped on the ledge, something pricked him and darkness engulfed him.

Chapter Eight

He was a distressed man when he arrived home. He did not know what he would do and what would happen to his children. It was as if his entire world had crumbled down. He tried calling his brother but he was not answering his phone.

"Is this how someone loses friends and people when they are faced with challenges?" he asked himself unable to hold the tears that were forming in his eyes.

He had found the house locked and it did not even occur to him that the children were not home. Everything about him had turned upside down. He slumped against the door. He cried his heart out. The pain was so much to bear and he wished Jennifer would have at least prepared him before she went. How was he going to handle everything? What was going to happen to his children?

"Or I should join you, my dear? There are people who are going to take care of our children. I cannot do it alone," he said after thirty minutes of crying.

"Who are you going to join, dad? Why should we be taken care of by other people?" Karangi asked as he watched his father crying at the door like a small child.

Kahiga was startled. He had lost track of everything and was not even aware he had any other person to take care of apart from his departed wife. He was not aware how long his boy had watched him. He was not even aware about what happened since he entered the young man's office at the hospital. The only thing he could remember was the discussion they had and then him telling him about the death of his wife. Everything went blank. He only found himself on a hospital bed. They later took him to view his wife's body and then he fainted again.

When he came to, they allowed him to go home to get someone to help him deal with the paperwork. He had even forgotten that. He had tried calling his brother from the hospital but he was not picking his phone. He had decided to go home and get him but then decided to check on the children first. When he arrived at his house, he had already forgotten what he had gone there for and grief overwhelmed him.

"Where were you and where are the others?" Kahiga asked as he stood.

He would not want his son to see him in his weakness. What he had witnessed was already too much and he felt a little embarrassed. He had to be their strength now that their mother was gone. It was going to be difficult, but he was going to do it.

"You did not tell me who you are going to join. Are you planning to leave us alone? Why is mum not coming back? We never get to see you often also. Do you go to see her? How is she?" the boy asked fearing that he would not be able to ask all the questions he had.

His father was not ready to answer all the questions at that time. He was not in the right frame of mind and did not even know how he was going to break the news to the children about what had happened to their mother.

"I am not going to leave you. I will answer all your questions later. Where are the others?" he asked his son.

"They are at grandmother's house. I am from there. She asked me to come find out if you had already returned. She needs you there," Karangi informed him.

"What is going on there?" he asked.

"I don't know but there are many people there. There is even a tent. I heard them say they are doing a watch, but no one has told us whose watch they are conducting," Karangi said innocently.

Kahiga was confused. How did they get to know about her and why would they place the wake there? It was not even appropriate. They should have waited for him before making such a significant decision. Why did his brother not see it fit to inform him about it? He did not even get the chance to correct his son. Emotions ran high and he was not in control of his faculties.

"Let us go there," he said beginning to get angry.

"Are you angry with me?" Karangi asked him noting his change of tone.

Kahiga bent and faced his son. He held him in his hands and talked calmly with him. He was so much stressed and did not want his children to be affected by whatever he was going through. The pressure was getting too much for him and he was wondering if he was going to be able to handle it.

"No, why would I be angry with you my son? I am just going through a lot but I am not angry with you. Let us go to your grandmother's place," he said as he caressed him lovingly.

They walked in silence up to his mother's home. His mother and his brother had a lot of questions to answer. He still did not have any idea how they got to learn about his wife's demise. They would answer all the questions when he got them. He still needed to go back to complete paperwork at the hospital and had gone to seek for assistance since he was not in the right state to do the paperwork. Had they learnt about it and cleared with the hospital? Everything was really too confusing.

More shock was to find him when he arrived at his mother's place. He found the tent erected as his son had told him and there were people gathered in the compound with shocked expressions on their faces. They were discussing in small groups. A solemn air hang over the place. When the people saw him, they stopped their talk and looked at him empathy written on their faces. Whether they were genuine or not, no one could tell, but they were genuinely shocked, probably by the vanity of life and the shortness and uncertainty of it.

"We are sorry about what happened, but God is in control," an old woman said in greeting to him.

"It is alright. Where is my mother?" he asked.

He was still wondering how they got information about his wife. He did not know how to confront his mother and brother when he saw them. They should have waited for him before making the decision to hold the wake for his wife in his mother's compound.

"She is in the house? She is waiting for you inside," a lady in her forties told him.

"What about my brother? Is he with her?" he asked trying to control himself.

The people under the tent were shocked. Had he gone mad with shock. How could he ask such a question? They thought that he knew what happened to him. Maybe he was still in shock.

"It is all going to be well. Go and talk with your mother. She needs you now," the old woman said.

He did not inquire further from them. He went into the house and found his mother with a strange man. She looked completely shaken and the man seemed to be explaining something to her.

"It is going to be hard processing his compensation. It appears the vehicle was not properly insured, or rather, the insurance company under which the vehicle was insured is now bankrupt and hence the cover is invalid," the man said as Kahiga stormed into the room.

"What are you talking about? Mother, are you still following up on the benefits after all the lies they have told us and selling some of his properties. What did I tell you? We should forget about his benefits and manage what he left behind. And another thing, what has it got to do with a motor vehicle insurance cover? All these people are the same. They will lie to you that they are working on your case but all they want is money," he said angrily.

"You, get out of here before I do something I am going to regret," he said referring to the man.

"I will come back when he has calmed down. He is not in a proper state of mind," the man said moving towards the door.

"Don't go yet. Wait outside, I will try to calm him down and impart sense into him," Kahiga's mother told the man.

"Alright," the man replied as he closed the door behind him.

"What is going on here?"

Kahiga was finding it hard to control himself. He did not want to disrespect his mother. His brother was nowhere in the compound. He wondered if his mother had made the decision on her own.

"Please sit down, my son," the woman said.

"I am not happy with everything that is happening, mother. You should have considered my feelings before making some of the decisions," Kahiga said taking a seat next to his mother.

"It is okay, son. I know you have been going through a lot and despite that, calamity did not find it imprudent to hit us," the woman said sadly.

"Who told you about it, mother? How did you decide all this without involving me?" he asked trying to control himself.

"We have looked for you the whole day. No one could get to you. We thought you would come back home early today after you heard what happened. We could not contact you to inform you but we thought you must have heard about it by other means. How is your wife doing? I should not be troubling you with so many things. I have not been able to go see her since yesterday. I was planning to go today then all these happened," his mother tried to explain.

"What are you talking about, mother?" Kahiga was almost exploding with shock and horror.

All the while, he thought they were holding the wake for his wife in the compound. What else had happened that he was supposed to hear about and why hadn't anyone told him about it?

"My son, I don't know what we have done. We would repent and atone for our sins if we knew what we have done wrong, but now where do we even start?" the woman said unable to control her tears.

"Please stop talking in parables, mother. What happened and why are all these people here? I thought everyone was here about…"

"About what my son? Haven't you heard about your brother? Don't tell me your…"

They both could not take any more. The old woman let out a loud scream and fell to the floor. Kahiga, on the other hand could not process what his mother implied. He felt light and also fell beside his mother.

Chapter Nine

After her friend's suggestion, Janet started thinking hard. She had been working hard to help the people through her organization. She even relied on social media as well as other media to raise funds for her philanthropic work. But there was one thing she was ignorant about; what the people went through daily as they tried seeking services from the institutions that were meant to serve them. Her status got her to move almost everywhere without queueing for anything. It was not so with the rest of the population.

"Ashley, this whole thing has got me thinking. If it were not for what happened to me and my finances, I would not have discovered the problems many people go through in their daily lives. I think before we claim to help people, it is important to find out what they need rather than give them what we think they need. I have come to realize what we do most of the times is to please our egos and feel good within ourselves that we are doing something for the people, but do we really know what they are going through?" Janet asked her tone full of concern.

"Can we go to the canteen? I think there is something you have pointed out that we need to address urgently," Ashley said as if Janet had awakened something in her that was asleep all along.

"But you know I am in no position to do that now. I have to go look for money to have my daughter treated. I have become like one of the people I have been thinking I was helping. It is not just enough to feel sorry for someone; it is not just enough to assume that whatever help you think someone needs is what they really need. One needs to go deep and form a relationship with the people. Feel what they feel and understand what they go through even if one doesn't experience it. I think we are deceived by our emotions and we end up pleasing ourselves but do not necessarily help the people we claim to be helping. In the end, the existence of problems and calamities seem to be what give us joy in life because they make us feel significant. If we were really genuine, we would seek to eradicate the problems rather than using people's problems to make a name for ourselves," Janet said.

"We are going to discuss this issue in depth later. For now, please take me to my father. I need to find out if he is going to lend me money for my daughter's treatment. About your idea, I just thought of something. If we informed the people about what I am going through, it will not even take a day to raise more than I need for my daughter's treatment. Can you imagine how many people out there who are suffering because of the systems just because they cannot raise money?" Janet asked.

"I get you my friend," Ashley said looking at her friend as if she was looking at an alien.

She did not know exactly what had happened, but it seemed the experience had really changed her. As she talked about her new discovery, she remembered incidences of her friends who had died or got paralyzed, not really lacking in finances to pay for the services they required, but not important and privileged enough to access those services on time and with the efficiency required.

"Get in the car then. There are things I need to tell you that will help the organization. I think you have a point in everything you are saying," Ashley said reflectively.

"I hope it is not another way of raising emotions. We need to work because there is need and a purpose to accomplish and not just to satisfy our emotions. People are suffering and we can't just use their suffering to caress our feelings. We need to identify the source of those sufferings and deal with them, even if it might not be easy and it might even cause us pain. We have to genuinely help the people by dealing with the systems that are causing their problems and suffering rather than taking advantage of their problems by creating foundations that only make a name for ourselves but hardly making any meaningful change in the society," Janet said.

"Alright, madam. I have heard you loud and clear," Ashley said trying to lighten the moment a bit.

"And what are you waiting for?" Janet asked as she took the passenger seat.

"Your wish is my command, madam," Ashley said taking the driver's seat.

"You can now talk. What is it that you wanted to say?" Janet asked as they drove from the parking lot.

"I wonder if the health insurance covers for the civil servants are really for their health or conduits for transferring money to people's pockets," Ashley said focusing on the road ahead.

"Why do you say so and why do you single out the civil servants?" Janet asked listening keenly.

"Maybe they are an example of what is happening everywhere, maybe not. But I have firsthand information about these schemes. They may be a replica of what is happening in every sector and probably reflect the rot in our system. I have several accounts I am going to narrate to you and you will understand what I am saying," Ashley said catching a glimpse of her friend to establish her reaction and then returned her focus on the road.

The first account involved a lady with eyesight problem. It had started with a little scratchy feeling on top of her left eye. She thought something had touched her and that the scratching feeling would go away, but when it persisted for three days she decided to seek medical attention.

"I think I should go to hospital and find out what is happening to my eyes," the lady told her husband on the evening of the third day after the problem started.

"What happened to your eyes, Phyllis?" the man asked.

"I don't know what happened. Maybe the doctor can explain. I just started scratching myself the day before yesterday. I thought it was something that was going to go away but it is getting worse," Phyllis said.

"Okay," the man said unconcernedly.

To him, that was the way of women, always creating mountains of mole hills. The only reason he entertained her talk was that he did not want to start an argument with her. How many people scratched their eyes and they did not make a big deal out of it. If his mother had gone to hospital every time she scratched herself, would they even have been born? It seemed that the woman just wanted to escape her responsibilities but he would not allow it. As long as he was the man in the house, she was going to obey his orders whether she liked it or not. She could go to all the hospitals she wanted to, but she had to carry out all her duties.

So, the following day, Phyllis went to the only hospital recommended by the medical cover. Based on earlier experience, she left home at two in the morning and by the time she arrived at the facility at some minutes to four, there were already people on the queue.

The doors opened at nine in the morning. Each one of them registered at the reception, the sole aim of the registration process being to establish if they were in a position to pay for the services they required or if their health covers were operational. After the registration, she was to face the rude shock that she would not be receiving any treatment that day.

"I am sorry ma'am; the doctor is on leave and will be coming back in a month's time. The facility has not been able to get a suitable replacement. He is the only optician we have across all our branches. So, I cannot refer you to any of our facilities but if it is urgent, I can refer you to a clinic we collaborate with. They will give you a discount and their charges are highly subsidized. They do not take your card though," the man in the doctor's office said.

"It is okay, as long as I am going to receive treatment and have my eyes well," Phyllis said.

She was referred to a clinic a few meters from the facility. When she went there, her woes seemed to be just beginning.

"We are sorry, madam. Our machines are broken down and are yet to be repaired. We cannot help you for now but we can recommend some glasses for you and later you can come for checkup when the machines are repaired," she was told.

"What is going on? Did we lose our medical allowance just to receive substandard treatment?" Phyllis lamented.

"You cannot talk like that, madam. These are just normal occurrences and they are going to be rectified," the lady at the reception countered.

"So, you are saying she lost her eyes?" asked Janet shocked.

"Yes," Ashley replied.

"How?"

"After many claims and visits to different facilities which they referred her to, her eyesight got weaker and one day she woke up and could not see anymore. When her family eventually decided to seek treatment from a different hospital that specialized in eye care, but which did not take her cover, it was already too late. There was nothing they could do with her eyes and she was forced to register with the visually impaired society. Right now, she is learning braille," Ashley said, her tone sorrowful.

"That is very evil. Why couldn't the family sue the hospital?" Janet asked.

"Who would they sue and where would they even begin. They were made to sign many forms protecting the hospitals against any liabilities. Besides, the family had used up almost all the funds they had and the little remaining was used to deal with Phyllis' condition. They neither had the strength nor the funds for a lawyer. And many like her are going through similar situations and there is nothing they can do," Ashley said in a resigned tone.

"But there is something we can do," Janet said resolutely.

"What?" Ashley asked looking at her friend suspiciously.

"Let me talk to my father first. You will tell me the rest afterwards. We will discuss our role in everything that is happening in a quiet place," Janet said as she ran to her father's study.

Ashley left the key to the car with the guard who parked it at the parking slot for the visitors. She was ushered into the living room by the maids who served her with white chocolate and bread.

Chapter Ten

A heavy cloud of sorrow engulfed Karangi's home. When the people outside saw mother and son unconscious on the floor, frantic efforts were made to get them to hospital. How could one family face so many calamities at the same time?

"It seems they committed a sacrilege and they did not atone for it. We need the elders to perform a ritual in the home to ward off evil spirits, otherwise, everyone will be gone in this home," a woman said as they placed Kahiga's mother in the car beside her son.

Two men joined them and they rushed them to hospital. Kahiga was the first one to regain his consciousness. He looked at the people inside the car with dreary eyes.

"Where are we going?" he asked.

"What happened in there?" the men asked.

Before he could answer the men, he saw his mother unconscious beside him.

"What is happening to us? How are we going to deal with the demise of two members of the family on the same day and then this?" he asked pointing at his mother.

As he was talking, his mother also came to. She looked around and began screaming. The driver parked by the roadside and allowed the two to calm down.

"Kahiga, tell me it is not true. Your wife is still alive," the woman cried to the shock of the occupants of the car.

They only thought that they were dealing with the death of Karuri, but there they were learning of yet another demise in the same family. How were they going to handle everything?

"It is true, mother," Kahiga replied holding his mother, trying to console her.

"What are you saying, Kahiga?" one of the elders who had joined them asked unable to comprehend what the man had just said.

"It is true. My wife died today at around one. I was coming home to get my brother to help me complete the paperwork so that we can transfer her closer home. I could not get hold of him on the phone and only got to learn of his demise in a most crude way when I got home. My mother informed me about it as I was informing her about my wife. I guess it was too much for us to handle. I don't know what happened afterwards," Kahiga said crying uncontrollably.

He could not hold the grief inside anymore. It was going to kill him. He decided to do the unmanly thing, according to the customs, and clear his system.

"It is already too late. What is the time now," the elder asked realizing darkness had already set in.

"It is half past eight," one of the men with them in the car replied.

"We will go to the hospital tomorrow and do the clearance. Let us go back and discuss how we are going to handle this situation. All the elders of the village and the clan need to be present. Hope they have not yet left," the elder said as the driver reversed the car.

Meanwhile, advocate Lennington was talking to a blind woman in the tent. He could not leave the place before he secured the deals. Another bird might swoop in and take the deal from his beak.

"I am advocate Lennington of Lennington and Sons Inc. Why are you sitting here all alone?" he asked in greeting.

"Pleasure to meet you Lennington, I am Phyllis. I just lost my eyesight because of medical negligence," the woman said extending her hand.

Lennington could not believe his luck. He went to the place to secure only one case but it seemed he would secure three already. How lucky could one be? He would wait for the two invalids to come back home. It looked like they held his destiny.

"Advocate Lennington, it is a pleasure to meet you ma'am," he said shaking her hand firmly.

"I think I could be of use to you. Do we discuss it here or do we do it in my office? I will organize for someone to pick you if you give me your address. They can do it tomorrow. We cannot allow rogue individuals to continue making the people suffer," Lennington said pleased.

"I do not have the money to pay for your bills. Please let us leave everything to God. He will make them pay for their sins," Phyllis said.

"How can you say that? I am here for that purpose. God chose men to the work. The powerful can only be dealt with by men like us. I am not going to charge you anything for the case. After you are settled, then you can pay my bills. I would not even call it paying, but saying thank you. I do not charge my clients," Lennington said excitedly.

"How can I believe you are true? No one takes cases for free just like that. There must be a catch somewhere," Phyllis said a sense of doubt clouding her speech.

"Let us say I am sent from heaven to help the weak in the society attain justice. I do not shout much since I only do it to help. So, you may not have heard about me, but I promise you, you will receive justice for what they have done to you. This is not the first case I am taking. I am here to help the people, and until my time is up, I will make sure everyone receives justice," Lennington said excitedly.

"I don't think this is the time and the place to discuss everything. How about we wait until all this is over. This family is in mourning and I am sure you could be of help to them as well," Phyllis said moving away from the man who was getting too close for her comfort.

"In fact, that is the reason I am here. I am going to take all your cases and believe me, justice will be served to all," Lennington said.

He wished his mother was still alive. He could have shared with her the good news. Though he did not believe in her God, at least there was something that was working to prove his existence. Otherwise, whatever was happening that day could not be attributed to luck. There must be a power somewhere connecting the lines for him. It was mysterious how he happened to hear about the man and how he responded when the other lawyers dismissed the case. He was sure he was going to win the cases and make it big in life. Too bad he could not follow the moral principles his mother taught him, and also that he had to keep away from that power that was guiding him. Though he was taking the cases, he was doing it all for himself but not to help the people involved.

The group that left for the hospital arrived back at a quarter past nine. There were still people in the compound despite orders from the authorities that no wake could be observed beyond six on account of security concerns in the region. The chief who was supposed to enforce the order was also among the people. What had happened at Karangi's home was not a simple thing. It could break every other protocol.

Among the people in the gathering were the elders of the villages, the local pastors and prophets, and administration officers representing the government. The group met inside Karangi's house. They were joined by the lawyer who had by that time made his name known among the important people in the village.

"Before we can go on, I wish to give this chance to Kahiga to explain to us what happened. We already know about Karuri, but it is good to hear from the family first," the chief said opening the meeting.

"Excuse me, chief Nani, before we move on, I suggest we form a committee that is going to organize all these things so that everything can be done formally," Lennington interjected.

Everyone looked at him suspiciously. Who was he to intrude in such an important matter. He was not even a member of the clan, not even a member of the community. But everyone seemed to agree with him.

"We are going to get to that," the chief said brusquely.

He was aware of what the man wanted and he was not going to make it easy for him. Though the family needed representation, he already knew him as a rogue man who had swindled the many people that he was representing. He was not going to allow Karangi's family to fall into his trap. Not if he could help it, though they had a right to choose whoever was going to represent them.

"Kahiga, please go ahead," the chief said.

"Thank you very much my elders, the government officials present and family members. We are indeed saddened by what has befallen our family. We never at any one time imagined this could happen to us. It still looks like a nightmare we are going to wake up from. We do not even know where we are going to hold the wake for the two who have left us," Kahiga said taking out a handkerchief from his pocket.

Before he could continue, they heard a commotion outside and had to pause and check what was happening.

"James, please check what is going on," the chief instructed.

James who was sitting close to the door opened it and stepped outside. He disappeared and left the others wondering what he had seen.

"We cannot abandon the meeting at this juncture. It is important that we make all decisions that have to be made in regard to everything that has happened to the family today. Kahiga, please check what is happening and don't disappear like the other man," the chief said.

When Kahiga got to the door, he was shocked by what he found. He thought that the man was outside the country. That was what they had told him when he went to his office. How could people be so hypocritical? When he needed him, he was nowhere to be found, but now that he had got a chance to make a name for himself, he shamelessly showed face in the compound.

"It is nothing," Kahiga said as he resumed his seat.

He had never been so disappointed with someone as he was then. He wished he could chase him out of the compound but he realized it would achieve nothing but unnecessary scandal that would interrupt what they were planning.

"Then why did James disappear?" the chief asked.

"We can go ahead with the meeting," Kahiga said not wishing to talk about the man.

"What is going on with you?" the chief asked.

He realized that the man was in distress. He had so much to handle and he was indeed taking it strongly, more than he would have expected, but even the strongest do have their weak points. Not many people could handle whatever the family was facing. The mother was not doing that well though. She looked lost in thoughts and very weak.

"I think it is important we discuss what we should do about what has happened to this family," Kahiga said impatiently.

"Calm…"

Before the chief could finish speak out he wanted to say, someone knocked on the door. James entered followed by the area member of parliament, with his PA closely behind. Everyone in the room, except Kahiga and his mother, stood to honor the man and gave him the most important seat in the room.

After he had sat, Kahiga did not allow him even to say a word, to the shock of everyone in the room. He continued to narrate everything that had taken place ever since his wife was taken ill. How she died without receiving any treatment because he could not afford the money they needed for her treatment. He narrated how he visited the constituency office but could not get any help. No one interrupted him. They understood what he was going through. The MP and his PA were frothing with anger though, but they could not show it. They would do damage control later.

From the corner where he sat, Lennington was taking notes, his excitement rising as the man continued the account. How many cases to handle now?

"One, two… four cases and counting," he made a mental note as excitement rose in him.

Chapter Eleven

Ashley had barely finished her coffee when she heard noise upstairs where Janet had gone to talk with her father. She stood to go and find out what was going on but the maids warned her against it.

"Don't dare if you care for your life. He is not going to do anything to his daughter, but as you can tell, he is not any bit pleased with her. I wonder what she told him," the maid said looking expectant.

"What if he hurts her? We should do something. I don't think everything is going well over there," Ashley said worried.

"Don't panic, nothing is going to happen to her. By the way, what is happening with your friend? If I understand well, she had sworn that she would never come here again," the maid asked ready for gossip.

"I don't think it would be prudent to talk about my friend to anyone. If she wants to tell her issues to anyone, she will do it herself," Ashley said indifferently.

"You don't have to be rude to me. I was just asking out of concern," the maid said disappointed.

"Then mind your own business," Ashley advised.

Janet stormed out of the room and banged the door. The old man came out and holding the door with one hand, shouted:

"Never ever consider yourself my daughter again. From now, I am going to treat you like a stranger," the man said and locked himself in the study.

"I never want to be called your daughter ever. I consider myself an orphan henceforth," she said crying.

Ashley rushed towards her, a worried look on her face. Whatever happened in that room, it must have been terrible. She never thought whatever Janet wanted to tell her father warranted such a commotion. Something else must have transpired and she was going to learn it from her friend.

"Let us get out of this place, Ashley," Janet shouted before she could even reach her.

At the car, Ashley could not bear the anxiety. She looked at her friend who waited for her to unlock the doors. Ashley stood looking at her and waiting for an explanation.

"Are you going to unlock the car or do I walk myself out of this place?" Janet asked angrily.

Ashley did not wait another second. Without asking any further questions, she unlocked the doors of her car and drove out of the compound.

"Why are some people so wicked?" Janet asked when they had got to the road.

"What are you talking about?" Ashley asked, though she knew she was talking about her father. She did not want to anger her any further.

"That man back there is an animal. I wonder how he even became my father. I wish my mother was still alive," Janet said sadly.

"What has he done?" Ashley asked focusing on the road.

"Can you imagine that he is the cause of all the woes I am going through and he has the audacity to demand that I help him in his evil schemes?" Janet said angrily.

"You need to explain to me clearly like a small child. I don't understand what you are talking about," Ashley said sincerely.

"I will tell you everything when we get to the city. There was something you were telling me earlier before we arrived here. Please complete it as I try to relax," Janet said leaning further back on the seat.

"Okay. As I was telling you, the systems seem to be completely rotten and powerful individuals are taking advantage of the situation of the corruption in our country to make profit from the people. They don't care about their health. All they are concerned about is money and how to make more of it. This explains why there are so many expensive vehicles on our roads and high-rise buildings are rising in our estates like straw houses," Ashley told Janet.

The next story involved someone who had a stomach upset, probably from some food she had taken. She went to a hospital along the road to the coastal region that was famous for making insurance claims that were both exaggerated and imaginary.

"I am afraid we have to admit you, madam," the doctor attending to her said.

"What did you say, doctor?" the woman asked in shock.

She had heard from her friends that people were being made to spend days in hospital so they could make higher claims, but she never believed it to be true. She could not believe she was experiencing it first hand and more so, it was involving her.

"I told you I just have a little stomach discomfort. Does that warrant my admission? I thought you would just prescribe some medicine and I would go home," the woman said.

"If you value your life, then you will agree to what I am telling you. We need to take you to the theatre tomorrow morning, Pauline," the doctor said without wincing.

"Are you serious, doctor?" Pauline asked shocked.

She stood up and moved close to the door of the small consultation room.

"The test results indicate something very serious and if we don't operate on you tomorrow, the condition might get worse. You might even die," the doctor said.

"Doctor," Pauline called but did not say a word.

"You only need to sign some documents here and we are going to admit you," the doctor said pushing some documents towards her.

"I need to discuss this with my husband first," Pauline said holding the door lock.

"There is no need to alarm him. Just sign these documents and then we are going to give you a bed. We will inform him for you. You just need to indicate his name and contact at the bottom of the last page of this document," the doctor said insistently.

"No, I need to make a call first. I will be right back."

Pauline moved out of the consultation room and called her husband.

"How long are you going to take. Yes, it serious," Pauline said.

"So, did she call her husband or what happened?" Janet asked shocked by the story.

"When she called her husband, she told him she was in an emergency. When she explained the situation to him, he told her to leave the hospital immediately. At that same moment, an expose was running on one of the mainstream television stations concerning the hospital. According to the report, the hospital had made claims amounting to hundreds of millions for services that were questionable. It also emerged that the hospital was forcing its patients to get admissions so that it could raise the bills. In addition, the hospital claimed to have conducted more operations than all the major hospitals in the country combined. That was besides claims of procedures it had carried out it did not have capacity to carry out since it did not own the required machines for such procedures. The hospital is under investigation now."

"And what happened to the woman? I imagine she is your friend," Janet asked.

"She is my neighbor, by the way. They went to seek for a second opinion from another hospital. You won't believe what she was told," Ashley said laughing.

"What was she told?" Janet asked.

She was not a woman who entertained suspense in her life. If you wanted to tell her anything, you did it there and then or never tell her at all. That was her policy and no one would win her over with surprises.

"Just a simple antacid was enough, imagine," Ashley revealed.

"When all these things happen, where do you think the authorities are? They can't just claim they are not aware of what is going on. You may be surprised that some of these big men are the ones who own these hospitals and they are board members of the insurance companies from where these claims are made. The one losing in this whole thing is the poor citizen who has no one to defend him," Janet said.

"You have a point there," Ashley said.

"Not just a point. I think we need to do something about everything that is going on. We cannot just watch as everything deteriorates further. We do not have another nation," Janet said in a serious tone.

"Now, tell me what happened back there with your father," Ashley asked.

"Do you know who owns the hospital in question?" Janet asked.

Janet was a master of suspense. She could keep you waiting for something until you gave up and there was nothing you could do about it. Many times, she would promise to tell someone something and then tell them to wait. When you asked her for what she was saying, she would have forgotten and you would be left wondering what she wanted to say. Ashley knew that and did not want to miss out on the information her friend had to share. She suspected that it had everything to do with what she was going through and also the information she had just shared with her.

"Who owns it?" Ashley asked expectantly.

"Guess it," she looked at her and realized she was not in the mood for such.

"Please tell it to me and if you are not willing to, don't keep me waiting," Ashley said point blank.

"Okay, you don't have to be harsh on me. You should at least give me some reprieve after everyone else and everything else has been so hard on me," Janet said.

"How do I help you when you always keep me in the dark? No matter how much I try to reach out to you, it appears you drift further from me and I have to keep on guessing what you want," Ashley said almost giving up.

"Are you now blaming me?" Janet asked.

"Please tell me what is going on. I really need to know so I can understand how to help you," Ashley begged showing frustration.

"Let me find out how my daughter is doing first and then I am going to tell everything to you," Janet said as she got out of the car.

"I might as well wait forever to hear it. Maybe I will get to know about it when they show that video in heaven, if we will get the privilege to watch it," Ashley mumbled as she watched her friend enter the hospital block.

Chapter Twelve

When Kahiga had finished his account about what had happened, the chief stood, looking reverently at the MP, he signaled everybody to be attentive and then said:

"We know that the MP is a very busy man. We are going to give him this opportunity and then we will continue with the agenda of the meeting."

The words cut Kahiga like a sharp knife on his heart. Given a chance, he would not have allowed that man and his people in the compound. He saw them as the reason his wife had died. They were just pretending to condole with them when they had failed him in his hour of greatest need.

"Thank you very much, chief Nani. As soon as I heard what happened to the family, I cut all my engagements to come and mourn with them. I know this is a very trying moment for the family. Kahiga, I am sorry to hear about what happened to your wife. If I had known earlier, none of this would have happened. I am going to sponsor a bill in parliament to make sure that this never happens again. We cannot be losing lives just because the hospitals cannot offer treatment to someone who cannot give a deposit. I am going to follow up on the matter and make sure that justice is served.

Mrs. Karangi, I know it is very hard to come to terms with what happened. But we have to accept the will of God in all things. I am really sorry. I am going to provide any support the family might need from me. Please do not hesitate to contact my office in case of anything.

I have other matters to attend to and I unfortunately have to leave. I will leave my PA here and he will update me on every matter that is going to be brought forward."

Kahiga felt like stopping him but he could not dare to. He knew how cunning and deceptive these people were. He had tried contacting him and the only thing he got from his office were insults, yet here he was pretending to feel sorry for the family. He was wondering why he wasted his time voting. These people who were meant to be their representatives had become their oppressors and looters.

"I will give my condolences today since I don't know if I will be available during the days of the wake. Please keep me informed about the date of the burial. I will be here to condole with the family. I know how hard it is to organize the burial of two people from the same family at the same time, but God is going to grace you. Here, is one hundred thousand shillings to aid in the funeral arrangements. Again, receive my condolences and feel free to contact me in case of anything."

He handed a bundle of notes to the old woman and requested to be allowed to leave.

"Where is the condolence book. I cannot leave without signing it," he said as he stood.

"We are just planning matters here. The book will be availed to you soonest possible. Someone will bring it to your office tomorrow," the chief said reverently.

"Please make it two books. We need to honor the two honorable members of our constituency," the MP said as he left.

As all that was happening, Lennington was taking notes. Still another case to take. His firm would have to hire more people to take over the cases. He mentally counted how much he was going to make and decided a little contribution would not dent his pocket that much.

As he watched the MP leave, he also made it a point to contest a seat during the next general elections. The honor the man had received was what he deserved. If he was as famous, they would not have made him wait for all that long. He did not regret the wait though. His patience had earned him four cases. He was sure these people were going to take him.

"I am also begging to leave. I will be coming tomorrow to guide you on the legal processes and I assure you that justice will be served in all the cases," Lennington said as he removed some money from his wallet.

"I am not as endowed as your MP. You know this country belongs to the politicians. My work is to help the less privileged in the society and I hardly get anything in return. Please take this to aid in the funeral arrangements," he said giving the lady a bundle of notes amounting to twenty thousand shillings.

As he gave it, he almost fainted. Though he knew he was going to recover it a thousand-fold from them, he still felt pain giving it away. But what could he do? He had to attract more money by displaying some.

"I will be leaving now. See you tomorrow."

"Thank you," said the chief dismissively.

He did not like the man any bit, but it seemed as if he was determined to get what he wanted. He did not know how he was going to stop him. He would try. He would rather get another lawyer for the family rather than have that swindler steal money from Karangi's family. But who was good among them? He felt it was better for the thief to come from among the people rather than from outsiders. At least with a looter from the community, the loot would go back to the people.

"I think it is now time to appoint a committee to guide us in the funeral arrangements," the chief said.

When the committee had been appointed. Everyone agreed that the chief should chair all the meetings. Though he refused it because of the nature of his job, everyone convinced him that as a friend of the family, especially the greatest friend of the old man, he should take that honor.

"I think we can adjourn the meeting for today and meet again tomorrow after the hospital. Did we agree who are going to help Kahiga with the clearance?" he asked.

"Not yet," a man in the group said.

"Joram, as the leader of the clan, I suggest you go with him to the hospital. You will be accompanied by Gachuki. I think those will be enough. And another thing, we will need a vehicle to transport the body. Mr. Chamiti, would you mind accompanying them to the hospital, your car will be fueled and something will be added on top," the chief asked.

"I am afraid not, tomorrow I will have to travel to the border town. But I will assign a driver for them. I suggest Mr. Saiti to accompany them."

With that agreed, the meeting ended and the rest of the people left Kahiga with his mother. They still had to agree how they were going to conduct the wakes and conduct the burial so that when they met the following day, they would have something to guide the committee.

"Now that what has happened has happened, we have nothing to do but accept it," Kahiga's mother said.

"It is true mother. I still cannot believe it has happened to us. I don't even know how I am going to break the news about Jennifer's death to the children," Kahiga said sadly.

"Leave that to me. I am going to tell them. You do not have to worry. You seem to forget I studied psychology before I met your father," the woman said.

"Thank you very much, mother. This whole thing is weighing heavily on me," he said.

"I understand. It is not easy on any one of us, but we will carry on through it," the old woman said.

They agreed that the wake be conducted in his mother's compound. However, Jennifer would be buried on Kahiga's land while Karuri would be buried on his strip of land in the family land. Too bad his wife had left him. They hoped she would not create a scandal during the burial.

"I have a busy day tomorrow. I need to go, mother. Please try to get some rest," Kahiga said

As he went to his house, he reflected on the events of the day. They were so horrible and he wished he was dreaming. He cried along the way as he walked alone. When he arrived in the house, he found out that someone had broken into his house and stolen his household items.

"What do you want with me?" he cried out loudly.

It was good he had left the children at their grandmother's. He entered the house and used a stone to close the door. He did not have time to inform anyone about the theft. How could people be so evil. They did not even care about those who were mourning.

In his bedroom, the mattress was missing. He was feeling tired. He went to the children's bedroom to rest there. He would find out exactly what they had taken the following day. He was lucky they had not taken anything from the children's bedroom.

As he slept that night, he had a strange dream. A pack of hyenas were chasing after a woman. The woman was carrying something that was very important to the people but the pack of hyenas wanted to get it from her. The people seemed to be angry with her and were on the side of the hyenas. She was about to be caught by the animals and the people wanted to feed her to them when he stepped forward and defended her from her attackers.

"They are not going to harm you. I am going to protect you," he told the woman as he held her in his hands.

"How can you protect me when I have done you so much harm?" the woman asked.

"What are you talking about?" he asked her as he tried to defend her from the pack that was drawing near.

"You will never understand. You should just allow them to punish me. I have harmed you and don't deserve your protection," the woman said.

"Forget it. I failed someone before, I am not going to fail you. I will defend you with my life if that is what it takes," he told her.

He lifted the woman and placing her on his shoulders, started running towards the swamp. It was the only place he could think of to safe himself and the woman from the people and the pack of hyenas that wanted to kill her.

"Please hold on," he requested her as he dodged the stones the people were throwing at him.

"Kahiga, Kahiga, have you forgotten we have an assignment today?" someone called him from outside.

He opened his eyes slowly. He was sweating and his entire body was drenched in sweat. His body felt numb and he felt something had happened to him though he could not tell what.

"What are you doing here?" he asked Joram when he had woken up and removed the stone from the broken door.

"How can you ask that? What happened here?" Joram asked assessing the situation.

"I think someone broke into the house," he said ushering the man inside.

"Karangi, Karangi," he called out but no one answered.

"I think you need some more rest. You left Karangi at your mother's," Joramu told him pitying him.

Then everything flooded on him. He panicked and grief took over his heart again. He looked at the empty house and wondered how he was going to cope with everything.

"The rest of the people are gathered at your mother's house. Please prepare fast and get us there," Joramu said as he left for Karangi's home.

"I will be there within no time," Kahiga said as he took his towel and went to the bathroom.

After he had changed to new clothes, he walked the path to his mother's house. His body felt heavy and as he looked at the green fields, he lacked the meaning of life.

"Jennifer, why did you have to leave me like this? How am I going to survive all these? Who is going to take care of the children?" he asked as he lamented.

"I think he is going mad," a woman who was cutting fodder for her cow told another standing by the roadside.

"What do you think is happening in the family? All this is not normal," the other woman said.

"I heard that his father took money from a very poor man and the man cursed him. I think that is why they are going through this," the woman cutting fodder, Karendi, said looking at Kahiga.

"No wonder they are facing all these calamities. I told Nyakio that all this was not normal but she did not believe me," said the woman on the road.

"Ssh, he is going to hear you," Karendi said.

But it was too late. Kahiga had heard everything they had said. He angrily approached the women. He held the one who was on the road by the fence by the collar of her blouse and grunted.

"What are you saying? Do you want to join them wherever they have gone?" he asked unable to control his anger.

The woman was so shocked to say a thing. Karendi on witnessing the scene dropped the machete she was using to cut fodder for her cattle and started screaming as she run towards Karangi's home.

Within no time, several people gathered at the scene and were shocked to see Kahiga strangling the woman.

"Please calm down, Kahiga. You cannot do this now. What has she done?" someone asked him from the crowd that had gathered.

"Please leave her. Remember we have to go somewhere," Joramu begged when he arrived at the scene.

Chapter Thirteen

When she arrived in her room at the hospital, the bed was empty. Where could they have taken Daisy? She checked her watch, it was five minutes past ten in the evening. Could it be that she had gotten worse and they were forced to take her to the operating theatre? But to operate on what? They had not even taken the courtesy to find out what she was suffering from until she paid them the deposit they were asking for. They just kept her on machines and cheap medications to maintain her life until they could start treatment on her.

"Could it be…"

That thought alone made her shrink. She slumped by the bed holding the sheets and started condemning such thoughts from her mind.

"No, Janet. You must be positive. Your daughter will grow to be a fine young woman," she consoled herself but she could not prevent her mind from exploring the worst.

At that moment, her friend arrived and found her crying alone in the room.

"What is wrong, Janet?" she went to her side and held her.

"Everything is alright, Ashley," she said still crying.

"Then why are you crying?" Ashley asked a shocked expression on her face.

The empty bed communicated everything Janet was not saying. She held on to her friend and tried to console her.

"It can't be. Daisy, what happened?" Ashley cried out.

"Please take me to the reception. We need to find out what is going on," Janet said rising up.

"What do you mean? Where is your daughter?" Ashley asked confused.

"Please take me to the reception," she said weakly.

They walked to the corridor, a few meters from the door of the room, at the far end of the corridor, they tapped on the shoulder of the lady behind the desk who was sleeping like she was in a hotel, on a comfortable bed.

"What do you want? Why have you woken me up this early?" the lady asked trying to adjust to her surroundings.

She was still sleepy and the bright light seemed to have been affecting her eyes.

"Oh, I am late for work."

Ashley almost laughed, but the gravity of the situation could not allow her to entertain such luxuries. She took a plastic cup from a pack on the counter and drew cold water from a dispenser that was connected to a socket on the wall on their left. She poured the contents on the lady who came back to her senses immediately.

"What did you do that for?" the lady asked when she had adjusted to her surroundings.

"You need to wake up and do your work. What do you think you are doing sleeping like that?" Ashley asked.

The lady shamefacedly looked at the two women and after drying herself with a towel she carried on her handbag, she assessed them and then asked.

"What are you doing here at this time? Aren't you aware that visiting hours ended long time ago?"

"And why are you alone here by the way? Does it mean that nothing happens here at night? Who takes care of the patients?" Ashley could not help but wonder.

"Please learn to mind your business. I asked what you are doing here, you are not in a position to ask me questions and what I do in my place of work is none of your business," the lady said rudely.

"I think it is more of my business than anyone else's. I need to be certain that I am going to receive the best of services where I or anyone related to me is receiving treatment. But, that is beside the point. Can you, please, tell us where the patient in room R305 is," Ashley said losing her patience.

"Why didn't you say that instead of creating a hullabaloo about nothing," countered the lady brusquely.

"Are you telling us or not? I think we should lodge a complaint against this facility," Ashley said.

"You can go ahead," the lady dared.

"Stop that," Janet shouted angrily.

These two were bickering without telling her where her daughter was. She did not care what was going on at the hospital and who was going to complain about who. All she cared to know was where her daughter was.

"And who are you?" the lady asked.

"Tell us what we want to know. What do you want to do if you get to know who she is?" Ashley retorted.

The lady was getting into her nerves. She wished she could do something at that moment. If it were not for her friend, she would have already taught the woman a lesson.

"Which patient did you ask for again?" the lady asked.

"Are you trying to play games with us, woman?" Ashley asked repeating the ward number.

"Oh, I thought you had heard about her. You are making noise as if you own the hospital or the ministry of health. What will you do with her body when you get to know about it?" the lady asked crudely.

Janet knees grew weak, her head turned light and she dropped to the ground unconscious. She hit her head on the edge of the couch that was a meter away from where she stood. Ashley let out a scream as the lady left the counter shock written on her face. She regretted her crudeness.

She had been going through a lot at that moment. They had not been paid for three months and her children had had to stay away from school for the best part of the time. Her husband who was working with one of the county governments had also not received his salary for four months. The landlord was threatening to send them out of the house if they did not clear the rent in the next three days. She had tried to do some hawking during the day since she was on the night shift that month, but nothing seemed to be working. She had realized that all her profits had been spent bribing council officials.

"See what you have done," Ashley shouted as she bent to check on her friend.

"I am really sorry. I did not mean to do it. Who is she?" she asked an apologetic expression on her face.

"The mother of the person you referred to as a body," Ashley said rudely.

"I am really sorry," the lady said.

"How is your sorry going to help my friend? Will you at least get some help," she said distressed.

She did not know what she would do if anything happened to Janet. She had been her life. She remembered that time she was chased away from her home by her father after getting pregnant with her son who later died. She was homeless in the streets when Janet approached her.

"Young girl, what are you doing here? Do you know that this place is very dangerous for young girls like you? Or do you want to get yourself killed?" Janet asked the young girl who sat on a sheet in a deserted street in town one evening.

"I don't have anywhere to go. My dad chased me away from home," Ashley said.

"Get into the car. You will tell me everything on the way," Janet told her as she opened the passenger door.

"Thank you."

She shared with her everything that had happened to her at home. How she had been defiled by a doctor who was also her father's best friend during a checkup. She explained to her how she had got pregnant from the incident and when she explained to her father what had happened, the father had chased her away from home claiming she was a prostitute who just wanted to tarnish the good name of his friend who was also a respected church elder.

"Why didn't your mother intervene?" Janet asked her.

"How could she intervene in such matters. She almost received a beating. He warned her that she would leave the house together with me if she said a single word in my defense. My father is this person who never listens to anyone and believes a woman's place is in the kitchen. Then, my mother is this quiet submissive woman who never wants trouble. She will try to avoid it as much as possible unless it finds her, and even then, she will run from it. She kept her calm and watched me leave with tears in her eyes," Ashley explained.

"That was very unfair. I thought such men did not exist in this century, and the last of them was my father. How mistaken I am," Janet said.

She had gone ahead to offer Ashley a place to stay. She facilitated her return to college to complete her course and would later employ her as the director of her foundation when she graduated. Since then, they became best of friends. They were more of sisters than friends. Janet had even gone ahead to reconcile Ashley with her father after the truth was revealed and reports of the doctor's immorality were exposed in the media.

"This is the most important person in my life. If anything happens to her, I am going to personally make sure you pay for it," Ashley warned her.

"Please help me get her to that ward over there. Everyone here is on a go slow since they have not received their salaries. Again, I am sorry about everything, but if we keep her here with this bleeding, whatever you fear will happen. You cannot blame me for that," the lady said.

The two lifted Janet and took her to the room the lady indicated. She stopped her bleeding and injected her with antidepressants and then they left her to get some rest.

She had been depressed the past few days and her body could handle no more. She had not even slept for the past three days and it had started showing on her. The news of her daughter's death took the last ounce of energy she had.

"I am sorry about how I treated you earlier. What is it that you were saying about not receiving a salary?" Ashley asked sympathizing with the woman.

"It is nothing. I know you must be stressed as well. By the way, I am Jackie. We cannot talk about it in this place, but I will invite you for coffee if you don't mind," the lady said as they both slumped on the couch at the reception.

"I am Ashley, I can't wait to have the coffee. I am sorry about how I behaved earlier. My friend is going through a lot and she isn't even sharing it with anyone. I have been trying to make her tell me some of it but she will always do what she wants when she wants it. You cannot force her to do anything. I am her best friend but I have to admit there is a lot I do not know about her. I can't believe her daughter is gone. There is something she wanted to tell me about her, she did not get to tell me even to this moment," Ashley said.

"I am so sorry about everything. I don't know what is happening in this country's health sector. It appears that health in this country was left for the rich and powerful. The rest of us, we contribute through the nose to secure our death. At that point, the system will be generous enough to give something to take you back to the ground where you came from and for the family to grieve before the next member departs," Jackie said.

"It is like everyone is becoming a philosopher. The situation in the land is making everyone a thinker, though there appears to be very few action takers and the situation is getting worse. How will we solve anything by talking?" Ashley asked reflectively.

"You talk as if you are not one of them. What have you done to change the situation?" Jackie asked.

"Jackie, why did you call me at this time of the night? What is the emergency?" a man asked from the door.

"Sorry, meet doctor Rahjeed. He is the only person who will respond when you call him. All the rest will not leave their comfort to attend to your emergencies. I called him when your friend collapsed," she told Ashley.

"Doctor, meet Ashley. She is a friend to the patient I called you about," Jackie said turning to the doctor.

"Pleasure to meet you, doctor," Ashley said standing to greet him.

"Please take me to her," Dr. Rahjeed instructed.

"She will be well. It is nothing serious. She just needs some rest and she will be good to go," he said after checking her.

"For how long should she rest?" Ashley asked.

"At least three days. She seems to have been through so much stress and needs to relax a bit. I would advise she takes two days here so I can check up on her," the doctor advised.

"I am afraid, that may not be possible," Ashley said.

"Why is it not possible?" the doctor asked.

He had realized that her vital organs were growing weak and if it was not checked it might turn to something serious. She needed to be helped on how to overcome stress and it appeared the environment she had come from was not conducive. Maybe she was working so much and she needed to rest. From what he had observed among his patients, they could only be contained in a hospital.

"She just learned about her daughter's death. She was in this hospital," Ashley said.

The doctor remembered the girl. He had begged the director to authorize the treatment of the girl but he had been adamant. He claimed that the hospital could not commence treatment until the guardians of the girl paid the necessary deposit. Her mother's health insurance cover could not be honored by the hospital. The girl's condition had deteriorated and, in the end, the girl had died of a condition that could have easily been treated.

"I am sorry about everything. I did not even remember the lady. I would advise the family to take good care of her and to help her organize the funeral. Right now, she needs all the support she can muster. I am going to recommend a therapist who will assist her. Please take her there after you have cleared with the hospital. I will call her and explain the situation," the doctor said in a sympathetic tone.

"Thank you very much, doctor," Ashley said.

"Another thing, please take her home now. If the director discovers that she has received any services here, it will be charged to her bill. Let this remain between you and me. I think it is a good thing that the staff has been on a go slow, otherwise we would not have checked on her," he said as he handed Ashley a card containing the contacts of the doctor he had recommended.

"Thank you very much. I will make sure she gets the therapy," Ashley said gratefully.

"Do you have a car?" he asked.

"Yes," she replied.

"Then we should take her out of here now. Jackie, do you have any problem with that?" Dr. Rahjeed asked.

"Definitely not," she said outrightly.

"Good. I don't think there is anyone else here. We will take the elevator. She will be up within an hour, but I don't want us to take any risks. We can only get her out when we have time," he said assisting the two women to carry Janet on a stretcher.

Chapter Fourteen

Kahiga realized that he did not know people at all. He thought he was a man of the people, but the situation that had befallen him made him discover what it meant to have people. They were waiting for the day you would get into calamity or have you or a member of your family dead so they could come to your aid. They had deserted him when he needed the money to pay for the tests the hospital required, but now she no longer needed the tests anymore, he received more than he needed for her treatment. They sent him so much money that he cleared with the hospital and transferred her body within hours.

They reached home at a quarter to eleven in the morning, having completed everything. The clan members and other people of significance had already gathered for the burial arrangements.

Among the people was Lennington. He knew he still needed to secure the jobs of representing the family in the various cases they needed to lodge to claim compensation for what had happened to them. Even the chief was shocked by his dedication and started having doubts about the stories he had heard about him. Probably, they were just rumors spread by people who were envious of him.

"There are several things we need to put in order. We will continue from where we adjourned our meeting yesterday," the chief said.

"Before we continue, I want to help the family legally so that justice can be served without further delay. The earlier we begin the process the better," Lennington said interrupting the chief.

"If I may ask, what are you asking for in order to take up these cases?" the chief asked testing him.

"As I told Mrs. Karangi yesterday, I only need the details. My desire is to see justice served for all. I don't ask anything more," Lennington replied to the consternation of the chief.

"What do you want now?" the chief asked.

"I was requesting if you could allow Kahiga and his mother to give me details of the case in private. I won't take much time. I need to go back to the city to start the process today. I will also need to meet another person from here. She suffered an injustice in one of the hospitals that made her lose her eyes. After I am done with Kahiga, I would also like to talk to her. I would appreciate if you could get someone to direct me to her house," he requested.

"That will be organized. Please do the best you can," the chief said beginning to respect the man he despised earlier.

"Thank you very much," Lennington said as they entered the house with Kahiga and his mother.

Lennington presented to them an excellent portfolio about himself. They were greatly impressed and wished they had met him immediately after their father died. They would have already got his benefits.

"You are really doing an excellent job of representation. If I may ask, if you do all these things for free, how do you manage it and how do you make money for yourself?" Kahiga asked to clear the doubts that were hovering above his clogged mind.

"God is ever faithful. Those who decide to pay me do so generously. And then, several humanitarian organizations support me when they hear about my work towards the less privileged in the society. But there are some envious people who have been trying to tarnish my name by sponsoring dubious investigations and media reports against me. I decided not to fight for myself but to continue with my work," Lennington said.

Kahiga remembered the great infamous swindler who had become very popular in the country three years before. For one year, reports of the people he had swindled emerged in the media. There was great outcry among the citizens and the investigative agencies put their foot to work. They promised to have the man compensate all those he had swindled and also put him behind bars for fraud. The case was a sensational issue for three months and then afterwards, nothing was heard about the man or the case. People forgot about him as new issues emerged.

"That was very wicked. I remember the reports and how the country bayed for your blood. Surely, God protects his beloved," Kahiga said convinced.

They explained to him everything that happened starting with his father's death and their struggle to get his benefits, they talked about Karuri's accident and Kahiga's wife death.

"About your brother, the case is going to be a little difficult since the vehicle that knocked him did not have a valid insurance, or rather, the insurance was valid but the company was not. As we speak, the company is under investigations, you know the way of investigations in this country. They will yap for some months and then the case will be forgotten. The government has placed the company under receivership but it is not yet in a position to honor claims that may be made against it," Lennington explained as if to a grade three child.

"So, what happens now? Does it mean that my brother's death will go uncompensated?" Kahiga asked.

"Not necessarily. I have evaluated the case and decided that we should follow the owner of the vehicle directly. In any case, the insurance company was bound to reject any liability against the accident since the driver was the one at fault in this scenario," Lennington explained.

"So, there is a likelihood he will be compensated?" Kahiga asked beginning to understand the situation.

"There is a very high likelihood, only it might take long. The court will compel the owner of the vehicle to pay. I have researched and discovered that the owners are a rich family. In fact, the father of the driver of the car is one of the owners of the insurance company in question," Lennington replied.

"What about my wife? You said there is something we can do," Kahiga said not willing to take too long in the house.

They had a lot to organize. Planning two funerals was not an easy task. Everyone relied on him and he had to support his mother the best way he could. She was completely shaken by the turn of events and if he was not careful, he might have another funeral to plan. He did not want that.

"About your wife, we are going to sue the insurance company and the hospital separately. The company for breaching its end of the contract and the hospital for negligence. This is going to be a monumental case that will raise the heat in the health insurance and general health in the country," Lennington said.

"I trust you are going to do a marvelous job. If you win these cases, you are going to get a lot of clients. Many of my colleagues are suffering and they don't know who to turn to for help. Some have lost their limbs because of medical negligence and malpractice. Misdiagnosis and greed for money have seen many being referred for treatments they do not need. In one of the stations, almost everyone was diagnosed with cancer and when they tried to investigate the matter, it was hushed up," Kahiga said.

"There are unscrupulous people in every field, but it takes a few people of integrity to call them out. We cannot tire from doing the right thing. We are going to win this battle against corruption that is killing our country slowly and restore the dignity of our people," Lennington said acting as the champion of the people.

"Thank you very much. I have full confidence in you. We have to go and deal with other things now. Is there anything more remaining to be discussed?" Kahiga asked.

"I think there is none. If you could sign these documents, then we would be good to go," Lennington said removing a bunch of documents from his briefcase.

They signed the documents and joined the rest of the people at the tent. Lennington went to discuss Phyllis' case at her home. He was a happy man when he left the village. By the time he was done with those cases, he would be a rich man and would prove his old man wrong. The man had said that he would not amount to anything in life.

"You took rather too long inside there. Hope everything has gone on well. Be careful about that man," chief Nani said as he welcomed the two back to the meeting.

"Everything went on smoothly. We are going to see what he can do. He is saying that he is not charging any fees for his services. I have signed the documents and he will go ahead with the cases. He is going to help us even recover our father's benefits," Kahiga said triumphantly.

"Did you go through the contents of the documents before signing them?" the chief asked.

Kahiga realized his mistake. He had not cared to check what the lawyer had written in the documents he had just signed. He had trusted him so much that he did not even think to read them through.

"No," he said worriedly.

"I thought you were a man of understanding. But anyway, there is nothing we can do now. The documents are already signed. Let us trust that he is a trustworthy man and he is not going to swindle you," the chief said.

"Let's hope so," Kahiga said the excitement he had earlier dampened.

"Let us go ahead with the meeting," the chief directed.

"We have discussed some of the important things. We understand that this is an unprecedented situation, but we have to go ahead with the plans since we cannot undo what happened. We have tried looking at the budget and came up with the simplest we could come up with. We considered the availability of finances and the responsibilities ahead after the burial. We were of the opinion that both Jennifer and Karuri be buried on the same day. It will help cut on the expenses. As for where they are going to be buried, we found it necessary to leave the decision to you. We were trying to look into various possibilities that would ease the conduct of the ceremonies and we have to admit it is going to be tricky to have them buried in separate places. Though your land is not far from here, we have to consider the fact that if we decide to bury them the same day, there is going to be a problem. You can tell us what you think and then we will work out the best thing to do in the whole matter," the chief said.

"Thank you very much. We are really grateful for the support you have given us since this whole thing started. We have no words to express our gratitude. All we can say is, may God bless you very much," Kahiga stated.

"Amen," they all responded.

"Concerning the budget, we cannot agree more with you. You have done your best and we are going to work with that, unless something else changes. On the burial of my beloved wife and my brother, we had agreed with mother that the ceremonies be held on the same day. However, we had not thought about the logistics of having them buried in different places. It is my wish that my wife be buried on my farm and I believe Karuri will be buried on the strip of land that belonged to him here. As for the wake, everything is going to take place here. What I am not sure about is how the ceremonies of the final day will be carried out," Kahiga explained.

"I think what we can do is to hold the ceremonies in one place and then the people separate into two groups to the grave sites. I believe separating the ceremonies is going to be so draining and time consuming that we would rather hold them on the same day," Joramu, the leader of the clan said.

"You have spoken well, sir. I think with that settled, we can go ahead with the plans. Kahiga, I suggest that you have your brother's body transferred to the same morgue you took your wife. It will make work easier. Three people are going to accompany you for that task," the chief said and the meeting was adjourned to the evening of that day.

Chapter Fifteen

They were almost five hundred meters to her house when she regained consciousness. It was a good thing that doctor Rahjeed had joined them, otherwise there was going to be a crisis that would have caused another catastrophe.

After driving out of the hospital, Doctor Rahjeed realized it was not going to be safe to leave the two women to drive home at that hour of the night. Besides, he did not know how Janet was going to react when she woke up. He needed to be there, just in case. He called Ashley through the number she had given him before they left the parking lot of the hospital.

"Please wait for me there. I am going to park my car at the petrol station and then join you. I don't think it is safe to take her home alone," he said as he drove towards Shell Petrol station which was a few meters from where he was.

He could still see Ashley's car as it meandered the corners of the road almost about to take exit nineteen. It would be safe to park there for some few minutes before he arrived. He was a quick walker and he did not want to make her turn back to get him. She would have been forced to drive to the next round about which was about a kilometer away.

"Where do I wait for you?" she asked relieved.

"Just park before the exit. I will be there in ten minutes," he said.

"Please, hurry before the authorities find me here and fine me for obstruction," Ashley said.

"I don't think they will be there at this time of the night, but I am almost there," doctor Rahjeed said locking the doors of his car.

Janet opened her eyes slowly. Her head felt heavy and there was a little pain. She touched an area on top of her head that was bandaged. She had no recollection of where she was. She surveyed her surroundings and saw a man beside her. She had not recognized Ashley who was on the driver's seat.

"Who are you and where are you taking me?" she asked calmly.

She did not want to think that they had kidnapped her. How could they be so cruel? The memory of what that rude lady at the hospital said was still fresh in her memory. She did not know what had happened to her or how she got into the car. She remembered Ashley and panicked.

"Where have you taken Ashley?" she asked worried.

If they had kidnapped her, then it meant they had also done something harmful to her friend who was with her. The man beside her only smiled. He had not expected her to be calm when she woke up, but it seemed she was responding well to the trauma that had hit her. He would find out more about it when they visited the therapist.

"I am here, Janet. How are you feeling now?" Ashley answered from the driver's seat to the consternation of Janet.

"Where are we going at this hour of the night and who is this man?" she asked confused.

"That is doctor Rahjeed. We are going home," Ashley said without explaining anything.

"What about my daughter? Where is she?" she asked beginning to get excited.

"I will tell you everything when we get home. Please relax and try to get some rest," Ashley said.

"Is it true what the rude lady said? I want to go back to the hospital. I want to be with my daughter," Janet said restlessly.

"We cannot go back there now. You need to get some rest. There is a lot ahead of us and you need to get rest," Ashley said firmly.

"No, I want to be with my daughter. They are going to kill her. Don't you understand? I want to be with my daughter. If you are not going to take me, then I am going to take myself there. Please stop the car and let me out," Janet cried.

"We are almost home. Please relax," Ashley said.

She did not know what to tell her. It was going to be hard to handle her in that state. Explaining about her daughter was going to be a dreadful task, but she had no choice. She had to do it.

"I am going to jump if you are not going to stop the car. Open this door for me or I am going to break the window," Janet threatened.

Doctor Rahjeed removed a syringe from a bag he carried and injected her with a sedative. She slumped on the seat and went back to sleep.

"That will calm her down for the time being," doctor Rahjeed said.

"Thank you," Ashley said focusing on the road.

They were now about two hundred meters from Janet's house. She could not wait to get there. She would figure out what to do when she got there.

"Are you married?" doctor Rahjeed asked Ashley.

Ashley was momentarily taken aback. She had not expected that question from him. She had not even thought about the issue at all. She dedicated her life to the organization and had no plans about marriage. Many men had approached her but he had turned all of them down.

"Why do you ask?" she asked indifferently.

Ever since that incident with the doctor, she had come to hate any man suggesting anything close to marriage. She did not detest men, but she hated the fact that they could imagine a relationship with her. Though she kept on pestering her friend Janet to get a husband for herself, she did not consider it appropriate to get involved in family matters herself. If what her father and mother had was what was called marriage, she would rather remain single for the rest of her life.

"I was just asking," doctor Rahjeed replied.

"No, but I don't think I want to discuss the subject," Ashley said tritely.

"Why?" doctor Rahjeed was not just going to let it go.

"Please, let us leave the subject. How do you think my friend is going to take everything? She still has not come to terms with the death of her daughter," Ashley asked changing the subject.

Doctor Rahjeed had started having a crush on the girl. He did not know how it began but something stirred inside him the moment he saw the girl at the hospital. He had not got involved with any girl in the entirety of his life. His family had organized a marriage with a girl whose father was his father's business partner. This happened when they were still children but he did not think he was going to honor the agreement. When he went to practice medicine in the popular East African country, he intended to break that agreement and even adopt the citizenship of that country. He had decided to remain celibate for the rest of his life, but this girl had aroused something in him that he did not know existed.

He did not want to anger the girl. He honored her request and decided to remain formal with her. After all, they had just met and it was prudent if they got to know each other before he proposed anything to her. He was determined to make her his friend and if possible propose an engagement leading to marriage to her. He decided to hasten the process of acquiring the citizenship of the country. He did not plan to go back home again.

"Your friend is going to be well. We will take her to the therapist tomorrow. She had had so much to bear and it is taking a toll on her. We can only hope that it is not going to break her. I can say she is a strong woman. Not many in her situation are able to go through what she has been through without breaking down," doctor Rahjeed gave his honest opinion.

"I hope she is going to be well," Ashley said worried.

She knew she herself would not have been able to handle half of what her friend had been through. She did not even know what she was going to do with her and was even expecting her guidance on how to handle everything. She was the only friend she had and every time she was going through something difficult, she would turn to her for advice. Now that she was the one in the tough situation, how could she then ask for advice from her on how to handle her?

"She is going to be okay," the doctor comforted.

"May I ask you a question?" he asked as the guard opened the gate to Janet's house.

"Yes, as long as it is not related to my personal life," she said strictly.

"How are you related to this lady? What did you say was her name?" he asked pointing at the woman beside him.

"Janet. She is my best friend, for lack of a better term to describe her. She is more than a sister to me," Ashley replied.

"I mean, is she your cousin, blood sister or any such thing?" he asked curiously.

"None of the above. Are you also interested in her?" she teased.

The guard had at that time opened the gate. She drove in as she looked at the perplexed face of the man from the mirror. She smiled when she saw his reaction.

What was wrong with this lady? Why was she being rude to him when all he wanted was to help them and be friends with her? She would come through soon. Her attitude harnessed his determination to get her.

The house was located in a posh estate in a suburb fifteen minutes' drive to the city center. It was gated with only seven five bedroomed mansions that were all similar. Each mansion had its own fence and a small gate for privacy. None of the residents was concerned with what the other did. The other inhabitants of the estate did not even know Janet existed and neither did she know of their existence, apart from the usual greetings at the gate as they got in or out.

Ashley parked the car in Janet's parking lot. It had space for two cars but was at that moment empty. She walked to the front porch of the mansion and opened the door. The maid who took care of the house had been on leave at that moment and Janet had not seen the need to recall her even after everything had happened.

"You are much welcome. This is my friend's house," Ashley told the doctor after she had settled Janet in her bedroom.

"Thank you," he answered politely as he took a seat facing the fifty-five-inch television.

"What can I get for you?" Ashley asked him.

"A glass of water will do for me," he replied.

"Coffee or tea?" she asked after she had given him water.

"I am okay. Maybe for yourself. You have had a long day and I presume you have not taken anything. You also need something to eat," he said caringly.

"Then I will make a light meal for us. But let me brew some tea. I understand Indians like tea a lot," Ashley said trying to diffuse the tension between them.

"You cannot make it as we do. Let me do that for you," he said moving to join her in the kitchen.

"You cannot do that," Ashley said shocked.

"And why not?" Rahjeed asked.

"Because…" she did not know what to say.

It felt odd but she did not know why it did. She watched him make the tea. She had forgotten that she also wanted to make a light meal. She was feeling hungry and Janet would also need something to eat when she woke up.

It was the best tea she had ever tasted. She looked at the man and wondered what was wrong with him. Something did not feel right about him. In her world, doctors were gods who could not perform ordinary duties, that was besides the fact that he was a man. They could not even interact with ordinary folk leave alone consume what they ate. She did not know they could even be that caring.

"Do you want me to make the meal for you? Tell me what you want to make and I will do it for you. You can take your rest. I know you must be very tired," he said as he went to the fridge to find out what was there.

Ashley was hypnotized. She just looked at him without saying a word. She was so mesmerized by him that she momentarily forgot who she was.

"Do you ever cook anything here? There is nothing in the fridge and the cupboard is as well empty," Rahjeed said disappointed.

Ashley did not answer. She just looked at the man like she was watching a movie.

"I will order something for us. What is this location?" he said as he removed his phone from the pocket.

Ashley was mute. She had started falling for the man without knowing it. She just sat there watching him. He noted her behavior and went ahead to pin the location for the rider who was going to bring his order.

He put on the apron that was hung on one of the wardrobes and started cleaning the utensils. Ashley did not know how to stop him. It was as if her body had been paralyzed.

"What is that man doing in the kitchen? What is going on, Ashley?" Janet asked as she opened the door to the living room.

Ashley did not hear her coming. She just continued watching Rahjeed. She moved with him as he placed one item after the other in their proper place.

Janet pinched her as she sat next to her and they both admired the man as he did his work.

"Why didn't you tell me you had a boyfriend?" Janet asked impressed.

"He is not my boyfriend. He is doctor Rahjeed. I just met him at the hospital and he assisted me to bring you home," Ashley said defensively.

"Check who is at the door," Janet said looking at her suspiciously.

Ashley went to the door and called out to Rahjeed.

"Doctor, are you the one who placed the order?" she asked.

"Yes, please sign for it. It is already paid for," he answered from the kitchen where he was placing the last of the utensils on the cupboard.

"Oh, you are up?" doctor Rahjeed asked as he returned to the living room.

"Yes, I am awake. Would you care to explain to me who you are?" Janet asked ushering the man to a seat opposite her.

"I am doctor Rahjeed. I am happy to see you are well," he said as he sat.

"Thank you. But you still have not told me who you are and what you are doing here. Is Ashley your girlfriend?" Janet asked like a strict mother who was protecting her daughter from marauding men.

"Oh, no. We just met at the hospital as I took care of you. I decided to help her bring you home since you were unconscious," he answered shamefacedly.

"Are you sure, you two are not hiding something from me?" Janet asked with the same strictness of a mother.

"What are we hiding? There is nothing between us," Ashley said as she placed the package on the table.

It was three in the morning. Ashley served the meal and they chatted for the rest of the morning until daylight.

Chapter Sixteen

After leaving Karangi's home and talking to Phyllis, Lennington went to his office to organize the cases. He could not believe that nature had been that generous to him. He decided that after he was done bagging the money from the cases, he would change his ways and start a new life in another country.

"God, I believe in you now. After this, I am going to change my life and dedicate it to you. Help me win these cases as you have helped me secure them for the sake of my mother who has so much trust in you. I am going to move to a new place and start life with you," he said as he went through the documents his clients had signed.

He was smiling as he thought about the prospects. How could one man be so lucky? Those who called him swindler would be shocked to learn the fortune he had amassed. He would make a mockery of them and pay them with everything they had done to him. No, he would be a changed man. He would start a new life, under a new name and in a new country. There was no need taking vengeance. His success was vengeance enough.

As he thought about it, the phone on his desk rang.

"Hello, Lennington? I understand you have taken that Karangi's case," said the voice on the other end of the phone.

"Who are you?" he asked worried.

Was it going to be so short lived. He had thought he had hit a jackpot. Who was that that knew what he was doing?

"That doesn't matter. Would you care to meet me in, let's say an hour's time at Safari Hotel in the city center?" the voice asked.

"For what?" Lennington asked apprehensively.

"I would say you need someone who will help you win your cases, if you know what I mean. At one o clock, Safari Hotel," the voice said and hung up.

Lennington locked the documents in a safe in his office. He took the elevator to the ground floor. His office was located on the fifteenth floor of Wayfairs Towers. He took his car and drove to the eastern side of town. He still had fifty minutes to spare. There was a man he wanted to meet there. If anything happened to him, that was the man he entrusted with all his secrets.

"What is it this time? You only look for me when you are in trouble," the man asked him when he arrived at his office.

He was a tall grey-haired man in his early seventies. He had been very instrumental in Lennington's career, teaching him all the tricks of the trade. He had shown him all the dark secrets that would help him avoid getting caught. He had been a judge when Lennington was beginning his career. He had introduced him to the most famous judges in the country.

"It is not like you think. You know I respect you a lot and I owe everything I have to you. This time I have landed a jackpot and I thought I should share the news with you," Lennington said guiltily.

He had not been to see the man whom he called his confidant for five years. When he succeeded in his career, he became so busy and did not see the need for the man who had made him rise. He was retiring at the moment he was beginning to secure lucrative cases. He held the man in high esteem however. The man did not take it against him though. He had learned from the best and it appeared he had become a very good student. He had always told him:

"People are there to be used. When you get what you want, there is no need to look back to those whom you used to get there. Never let anyone lie to you that you will need them again. When that time comes, there will be others to use. Always make use of every person that comes your way and make sure you get everything from them. Show no mercy at all. The world is for those who show no feelings and have no scruples about morality. When you excel, you will realize that everyone will honor you. It doesn't matter how you succeeded. As they say, the end justifies the means. Let the moralists cry as they continue suffering, your work is to succeed by all means."

"Then tell me why you are here. I know there must be something you need from me and I might be the only person whom you will never come to the point of doing away with," the man told him.

"I have bagged five important cases. One is going to be a monumental one. I cannot explain how I landed them, but as you say, there must be a power above and we must recognize that power. I managed to get them before everyone else and they are going to make me filthy rich. Of course, people are going to cry but my name will be great," he said explaining the details of the cases.

"What is in it for me? You know you can't just use me," the man asked beginning to get greedy.

"Definitely there will be something for you. But you have to play your part perfectly. You taught me that nothing is for free in this world," Lennington said.

"So, what will be my role?" the man asked.

"I will explain that later. I am here for a totally different reason," Lennington said.

"Shout it out. Did I not teach you never to beat around the bush? Always say what you want when you want it and stop wasting your time and the other person's time," the man reminded him.

"Someone called me asking me to meet him. I don't know how he got to know about the case but I presume he must be a powerful man," he explained.

"What did he say?" the man asked.

"Nothing much. He said I would need someone who would help me with the cases and then hung up. I have only fifteen minutes left to meet him. I wanted your advice on the matter," he said beginning to get impatient.

He wanted to arrive at the venue before the man. He wanted to be prepared for any eventuality. He could not afford losing the cases to anyone.

"Then meet him. I don't see anything wrong in meeting the man. Always remember what I taught you. If you follow that, you will always have power over everyone that you meet. Power belongs to the one who allows the others to play their cards first before they reveal theirs," he advised him.

"Thank you. I have to get going," Lennington said as he left the old man.

He had ten minutes to get to the venue. Taking into consideration the traffic at that hour, he would have five minutes to spare before the meeting with the strange man who had called him.

When he arrived at the Safari Hotel he gave the key to his car to the guard at the entrance to park it for him. He also gave him a two hundred shillings tip and climbed the stairs to the third floor where the restaurant and meeting rooms were located. He was always afraid of elevators and whenever he could help it, he would take the staircase.

He had barely taken his seat at one of the corners in the restaurant when his phone rang. He picked it up and was surprised to hear the voice.

"Look behind you, three tables from where you are," the voice said.

He looked behind. The two tables next to him were occupied by strange looking men. He was certain they were hitmen who would not think twice before taking away someone's life. On the third table, a man in a godfather cap sat smoking a cigar. He was the notorious PS. Even after he had left government service, people continued referring to him as PS. He panicked.

"Are you surprised? Please come and join me," the man said laughing impishly.

Lennington slowly went and sat opposite the man. He did not stop smoking his cigar as he blew smoke towards Lennington. He still maintained the fearsome expression he had when he was with the civil service.

"How are you doing, my friend?" he greeted as he placed the cigar on the table.

"What do you want, Skunka?" Lennington asked following the rule of his mentor.

He did not want to waste time with unnecessary chat. He had learned that one principle of power was to always present oneself as a straightforward person who did not entertain empty rhetoric. He had realized that those who controlled others did so through manipulation. He was not willing to sit there to be manipulated.

"Why? Can't friends sit somewhere and have a cup of coffee as they chat their day off? It is not always business. Sometimes people need to take a break and look at the other side of life," Skunka said.

"I do not subscribe to that school of thought. There is no time for idle talk on the earth. Others will be taking your wealth as you idle away. Haven't you heard what they say, time is money? One can't waste money away idling," Lennington said trying to place himself on equal level with Skunka.

It was the only way he was going to negotiate something beneficial to himself. He had learned the business world, what the common man referred to as the underworld, operated on mutual benefits. The only thing one needed was to locate someone with similar interests as one's own and then take advantage of one another. Whoever overpowered the other would reap the benefits and the one who lost would wait for another day if he learned his lesson and lived to fight another day.

"I am not your enemy here. In fact, we are all going to benefit greatly from what I am about to propose," Skunka said adjusting his glasses.

"And what is the proposal? I am the one to decide if it is going to be beneficial or not," Lennington said firmly.

"I can see you have grown firm teeth since the last time we interacted. Hope you have not forgotten who rules the streets?" Skunka asked in a threatening tone.

"But there are rules for the streets and all of us fight by those rules. Everyone is looking to make it great and one chooses whom to work with. Those who wish to work with him and are unaccepted can look for means of getting into the deal or stealing the deal altogether. At least I have not chosen the players in this deal," Lennington said bravely.

Skunka realized he was not going to easily arm twist him. The deals he had got were very lucrative and he still wanted to use him to deal with an issue that was disturbing him.

"You are getting wiser every day. Now, listen to my proposal. I know you are going to sue the insurance companies, which you know I am a shareholder and we do have strong lawyers to counter you. These cases you have taken are very important and the government is somehow involved. You are going to become famous and I want to have a share of the chunk you are going to be awarded," Skunka said without giving many details.

Lennington understood what he was driving at. He was willing to cooperate with him if at all the deal he was going to propose was reasonable.

"The compensation amounts will amount to several millions but there are risks involved. You know it is very easy for you to lose your life in the process and there is nothing anyone can do. If you don't swindle your clients, they will be swindled by another. I am suggesting the best judge to handle the case. We will come with the best agreement if you agree to my proposal then as usual, the ratios of the loot. All of us are going to benefit. The people representing the companies you are going to sue do not care whether they lose money, what they are concerned about is how much they are going to get out of it. You know the cases will be good for their reports when the auditors knock on their doors," Skunka said boldly.

He knew there was nothing to hide. Everyone who was present in the room knew how things operated. Lennington was the master of the game and he knew too well how things worked. He had been a beneficially of such dealings on many occasions, though on a small scale. On this occasion, he was going to be the main beneficially and as such, the one calling the shots.

"I don't think there is anything wrong with what you are saying. Get on board, friend," he said pouring two glasses of scotch.

"To business," he said raising his glass.

He was afraid about how everything was going to work out. He had been afraid that Skunka wanted to set him up and take away everything from him, but from what he had said, he meant well for him and he was going to reward him for his trust.

"There is another favor I want from you," Skunka said putting his glass down.

"What else?" Lennington asked.

He had already calmed and was getting very hopeful about everything. Everything was working according to plan. He looked at the man before him and was happy that he got to know such men. They represented power and wealth. Whoever was on their good side was bound to excel. However, those who were on the other side would never live to tell the story. One could get to the wrong side any minute and without warning. At the moment, he was on top of things and the man needed him. That was a plus for himself, though he could not lower his guard any moment.

"One of the cases involves my rebellious daughter. I want us to fix her and I assure you that we are even going to gain more from the deal. Much more than you can believe," Skunka said.

"I don't understand. I was thinking we could let the case go and set your daughter free. After all, winning three cases out of the four the family has entrusted me with is not something bad. They will be grateful," Lennington said curious to understand what he man wanted.

"Winning all of them is even better. I know you also remember it is not their win but our win. They are just the pawns we are using for our end. My daughter decided to go against me and I intend to strike a jackpot from her rebellion. I brought her to this world and if she becomes a liability, I have to look for ways to turn the liability into an asset," Skunka said.

"I get it," Lennington said.

"So, what do you want me to do," he asked the man who had all of a sudden become quiet as if he was calculating some missing assets from among his number of properties.

I will explain everything when we meet with the judge.

Chapter Seventeen

A heavy cloud of sorrow engulfed Gatweku village. Never before had they experienced such a catastrophe. Everyone wanted to go to the morgue to view the bodies of those who were to be buried. They wanted to confirm if witchcraft was involved and if it was, how such bodies looked like. They still could not believe what had happened.

"I think there was something going on between the two. How is it possible that they both died on the same day? One can never deceive the people and think they can deceive God. They are paying for their own sins," one of the women waiting for the hearse taking them to the morgue told her mate as they stood by the roadside.

"How can you talk like that? What if someone hears you? Some things we know but we keep to ourselves. I hear the child she was carrying belonged to the man, so it is not even two people we are taking to the grave but three. We can say, we are burying an entire family. I wonder why they decided to separate them," the other woman said.

"Let us be quiet so they do not say we are the ones who have invented the story. I am not afraid though, even if they know, it is the truth and we cannot keep on covering it up, the reason our village is suffering is because of covering up evil," the first woman said.

"If I was in the burial committee I would have suggested they just bury them next to each other," the other woman added.

By evening, several versions spread in the village and the villages beyond. One version claimed that the mother was involved in witchcraft and that she wanted to take away her daughter in law. In the end, she ended up losing both her daughter in law and son. The other version claimed that when the husband found out about the affair between his wife and his brother, he beat up his wife until she became unconscious. The brother, unable to handle the sickness of his lover who was on the verge of death, decided to commit suicide.

But away from the rumors, Kahiga learned a precious lesson about life. He would not have learned about it if the catastrophe that had struck them had not happened. He came to understand that people valued death more than life. He discovered that all the welfare groups that were formed were nothing but a means to securing one's death. Even the health insurance covers that one took concentrated on death.

When he needed to have his wife treated, no one came through for him, but when she died, even people he did not know contributed thousands of shillings for his wife's burial. The workers union also visited his home with their contribution and the insurance company that had made it hard for her to get treatment gave him a last sendoff cover that was more than enough to cover for all the tests the hospital had refused to carry out because he could not pay the necessary deposit.

As he cried in one corner of the tent holding his children who could barely understand what was going on, he regretted life. He started thinking about what he could do to make life more valuable than death.

"My sons and daughter, as you wade through the maze of life, please learn the value of life and guard it. I do not know who is going to teach you since no one taught us about it, but I believe you are going to learn by yourselves," he told his children as he wiped tears from his eyes.

"Father, what is going on? Why are you crying? We do not understand what you are saying," Karangi spoke on behalf of the rest. They were all crying.

"You may not understand it, but you are going to understand it later," he said a bitter feeling creating pain in his chest.

"Where is mother?" the daughter asked.

"Mother is gone. We are going to get her so we can place her in a hole. Do you remember what happened to the old woman at the corner? We are also going to do the same to your mother," he said feeling sorry for the children.

No one had taken the time to explain to them what had happened. The only thing they saw were many people who visited their grandmother's home every day for the past seven days. They were also staying there and they could not see their mother whom they were missing very much.

"But why? I want to be placed with her in the hole," the girl said innocently.

"That cannot be," Kahiga told her.

"You will understand it when you grow older," he said.

"But I already miss my mother," she insisted.

"Me too," the boys added in unison.

"Let us go. They are going to leave us," he told them as he tried to comfort himself.

They went to the hearse. At seven in the morning of Thursday 12th December, 2019, the family left to collect the bodies of their mother and that of their uncle, the brother to Kahiga from Lasjo Funeral Home.

*   *   *

It was a private ceremony held in the VIP area of the most famous public cemetery in the country. Only a few people gathered to give the little girl her last respects. The small white coffin reflected bright rays from the sun. The middle was darkened by an ominous shadow that seemed to blot out the bright rays.

Janet, dressed in a black silk dress and a black hat stood by the small coffin. Ashley who was also dressed in a similar outfit stood beside her holding on to her. They both were crying as the priest conducted the ceremony.

"It is such a painful moment when a young soul like Daisy's depart like this. Those who are left, especially the parents wonder what they did wrong. They cannot come to terms with the fact that a vibrant person, someone who would have grown to live a very productive life would depart so early. But I would like to encourage you with what David did when he learnt that his son had died. He said, that his son could not come where he was, but he, David, would find him where he had gone. It is very hard to understand why some things happen, but we have to accept them as they are as we seek the guidance of the Lord. Today, we lay to rest such a young soul. She will be with the Lord and we can only wait to be with her there when our time comes."

When they had just lowered the coffin, three police officers joined them. They would have almost interrupted the ceremony but Rahjeed prevented them.

"You cannot be so cruel. Whoever sent you here must have known what is going on. At least be human and allow the ceremony to end," Rahjeed said restraining the officers.

Janet and Ashley were so shaken to understand what was going on. The priest noted it but went ahead with the ceremony as if nothing had happened. He did not want to alarm the mother and ruin the ceremony.

After they had placed flowers on the fresh mound of earth, Janet and Ashley were walking towards the car followed closely behind by Rahjeed. He was trying to make the officers wait until Janet had settled from her mourning but they would hear none of it.

Janet and Ashley had not yet realized what was happening. When they saw the officers following Rahjeed, they thought that they had to guard the mourners against the muggers who frequented the cemetery. They continued walking.

"Can I talk with you aside?" Rahjeed requested the leading officer in a soft tone.

"Only a minute for you," the officer said.

"Why are you doing this?" Rahjeed asked.

"We have orders from someone very powerful. It is either we arrest her or our relatives will be clients of this place tomorrow, only for us we will not be privileged to use the VIP section," the officer said trying to make Rahjeed understand.

"Can't you wait until she gets home? She has been through a lot and I wonder whether she will be able to handle it," he begged them.

"I am afraid not. We have even gone against the orders and don't know what is going to happen to us when we meet our boss," the officer said pushing him aside.

"I am sorry, we have to do our work," he said.

"Janet, you are under arrest for the murder of Karuri Karangi and reckless driving. You have the right to remain silent, otherwise, whatever you are going to say is going to be used against you in a court of law. You have a right to a lawyer. If you don't have one, the state is going to provide you with one," the officer said as she stopped the two ladies.

Janet was too shaken to react. She looked at the two officers and just spread her hands before them. She was just tired with everything that was happening. She just needed rest. She did not say a word. They led her to their van, none of them saying a word to the other.

"Let us follow them in our car," Rahjeed told Ashley.

"Why are they doing this?" Ashley asked crying.

"I don't know. We will find it out at the station. There seems to be a very powerful person behind this," Rahjeed said.

"This is very unfair. Could they not have waited for her to mourn her daughter?" Ashley asked crying.

"This is no time for such sentiments. We need to find out how we can help your friend. Does she have a lawyer? Whatever is happening is unlawful and only a lawyer can stop it," Rahjeed said as they entered their car.

He hoped he would be able to follow up with the officers and that he would not lose them. They had not said which station they were taking her to. If they failed to identify the station, it would be very hard to help her.

"She does. The one who represents the organization. She is Damaris Nnabi," Ashley said in a panicky voice.

"Do you have her number? Call her immediately," he ordered as he drove fast trying to keep pace with the officers.

"I can't. Please dial it. I am so nervous," she said crying.

"Please try to relax and dial the number. Put the phone on speaker mode, I will speak to her. I can't lose them now," he said getting distressed.

"Alright," she answered her fingers shaking as if she was suffering from a strange muscular condition that interfered with the coordination of her muscles.

After ten minutes of struggle, she managed to dial the number and put the phone on speaker mode.

"Hello, Nnabi and Nnabi Advocates, how can I help you?" said a lady on the other end of the phone.

"This is Doctor Rahjeed. I am calling on behalf of Janet…" he hesitated.

He did not even know her second name. Her friend was so shaken to be of any help.

"Yes, Janet. Can I speak with Damaris?" Rahjeed said cursing through his teeth.

"I am afraid you cannot at the moment, but I can pass her your message," the lady on the other end said.

"Please, it is urgent. Try to reach her and tell her that Janet has been arrested. Tell her to reach out to Ashley when you get her," Rahjeed said.

"You said Janet who…"

The call had already dropped. He could not dial the number again. The police car was driving so fast that if he wasted any second, he would lose them. It was as if that was what they were trying to do, to lose him. He accelerated, not mindful that he would be stopped by the traffic police for speeding. He had one goal in mind, to establish where they were taking Janet.

At the intersection, traffic started building up. The officers put their siren on, and sadly, Rahjeed had no choice but to give up the chase as the traffic came to a standstill.

Chapter Eighteen

After losing the officers, Ashley and Rahjeed went to Kiston Hotel to decide the next course of action. They did not understand why the officers took her in that manner. It was strange that they did not even allow her to complete her mourning. They took her like a dangerous criminal who would run away or wreak havoc among the people.

"Do you know anything your friend has done that is so grave that they should take her like that? Are there people she has rubbed shoulders with and are fighting back against her?" Rahjeed asked when they had taken their table.

"I don't know anything she has done that could make the authorities treat her like that. I sense something fishy in everything. She is the kindest person I know and of unquestionable integrity. She had tried to make life easy and bearable for the less privileged in the society. She follows all the laws of the land. However, she knocked down a man with her car a few days ago and she went to the station to record her statement and do that which the law requires. Her car is at the station even as we speak. She has cooperated with the authorities despite the fact that she is in mourning. I don't understand what is happening," Ashley said and started to cry.

She did not know where to start to help her friend. She had no idea where the officers had taken her. She only prayed and hoped that they would not harm her and that they would release her soonest possible.

"There must be people who are not happy with what she is doing and we need to find out who they are and what they are specifically against," Rahjeed said.

"I don't know of any such person. The only person she quarreled with is her father and it was just family issues, nothing too serious," Ashley said.

"I think we should call her lawyer. We need to find out where they have taken her and the reason for her arrest. We will be able to know what is going on. That is the only way we can help her," Rahjeed said.

"What did she say when you called?" Ashley asked.

She was still shaken and was worried about everything that was happening. It was as if some evil had been released somewhere against Janet's life and it was determined to kill her. She looked at her phone and wondered what she should do. She could call her father and inform him about it.

"She was not in at that moment. I informed the receptionist to inform her about the incident. I think we should call her again so we can explain everything to her and she can advise us what to do," Rahjeed said.

"That is good. I think I should also call her father. He might help her. He is a powerful and very influential man," she said as she dialed the lawyer's number.

"Hello, Ashley. I got the message from my secretary. Where are you?" the lawyer asked from the other end.

"We are at Kiston Hotel, I am with the man who called earlier," Ashley said without giving too many details.

"And where is Janet?" the lawyer asked.

"We have no idea where she was taken to. We tried following the vehicle but we lost it at the intersection to town due to a traffic jam," she said.

"Okay, I will be joining you there shortly. Do you have any idea why they could have taken her?" the lawyer asked.

She understood there was something sinister going on. She had told Janet that if anyone approached her about the case with the accident, they should call her directly. That they arrested her raised more questions than answers. She had to do something and fast enough before they did something crazy. Many like her were being framed for crimes they did not commit just because someone wanted to accomplish something illegal. She was not going to allow Janet to become a victim of the justice system.

Everything was going south in the country and it seemed like everyone was on the brink of death, not of natural causes but death by design. Corruption had sucked out all the funds meant for services to the citizens. She was wondering how delegations could be sent outside to learn things that only needed action locally. Several times, she had witnessed delegations close to a thousand people sent to learn something that one representative could have sufficed. The wastage in the country was leading to so much suffering.

To cover for their mistakes, the officials were oppressing the citizens and so many of the systems were failing as a result of the incompetence. If something was not done urgently, many of the systems would require to be reestablished at the expense of the many people who were left suffering from the consequences of their inefficiency. For instance, the health system was in dire need of order and if something was not done urgently, only a catastrophe would awaken a people that was in limbo.

She arrived at the hotel twenty minutes later. She found Ashley and Rahjeed sitting quietly, each one deep in thoughts. Rahjeed was thinking about Ashley. The more he got to know about her, the more he was falling in love with her. He had made up his mind that he would not go back to his country. He would break any agreement made between his family and the girl he was supposed to marry. They could not dictate what he was going to do with his life.

For the time he had lived in the country, he had noted that the people were very religious. Though he proscribed to Buddhism back in his country, and hardly practiced any religion in the country, he would change to whichever religion Ashley proscribed to, just for her.

"Ashley, tell me what is going on," the lawyer asked as she joined them.

"I really don't know. We were coming from Daisy's funeral when the police came and took her away. We don't even know why and where she was taken," Ashley said still looking worried.

"What, Daisy is dead? And why didn't anyone tell me about it?" she asked genuinely shocked.

Janet had hinted to her everything that had happened at the hospital. She was drafting a charge against the hospital. She would advise her to sue the hospital for negligence. It was a pity that everything happened just as she was about to present a case to have the hospital treat the girl and drop all their demands.

"I don't know how it escaped any of us. I think there have been so many things. I don't know what is going on," Ashley said unable to explain a thing.

"Please tell me anything you know about Janet's daughter, the accident, the organization, and if there is any person she had quarreled with or who was following her. Tell me also about her arrest and the number plate of the vehicle the officers that arrested her used," the lawyer requested.

Ashley narrated everything she knew about Janet's predicaments. She explained how they tried to give a chase of the car that the officers used.

"I am sorry, we did not get the plate number of the car the officers used," Ashley said disappointedly.

"That's because it had no plate," Rahjeed added.

"Don't worry about it. We are used to that in this nation. I will try to make some contacts. We will establish where she was taken to before the end of the day," the lawyer assured.

"I have to get going. Keep me updated in case you learn anything. Thank you very much for the information. I will know what to do," she added and then left.

After she left, Rahjeed had made up his mind, he would not keep what he felt in anymore. He looked at Ashley and then excused himself.

"I have to get something from the shop three blocks away. Would you mind waiting for me here? I will be back in a minute," he requested.

"It is okay. I will wait for you," she said.

So much was going on in her mind. She did not know what to do about the situation that faced her friend. She knew it was affecting the organization a lot. She was afraid that she was going to fail her when she needed her most. With everything that had happened, there had been shortage of funds and most of the workers were yet to be paid their salaries. She did not know how she was going to convince them to be a little patient.

"I have to do something. I cannot fail Janet at this hour," she said to herself as she sipped the last drop of coffee in her mug.

"Please add me more coffee," she told the waiter.

"Yes ma'am," the waiter said and left to take her order.

She picked her phone and dialed her bank manager. She had saved some money in her account. It was not much but she believed it would go a long way in solving the crisis at her friend's organization. She knew that Janet would not approve of what she was about to do, but she came through for her when she was in dire need, it was her moment to do something for her.

"Hello, I would like to transfer some money from my account just right now. Is it possible to do it?" she asked hopefully.

"How much do you wish to transfer?" he asked.

"I will call you in a minute," she said and then hung up.

She dialed the human resource manager. She hoped that the figure she would be given would not be too high that her savings would not be enough to clear it. She did not mind if her account was left with zero balance.

"Generally, we pay around two million shillings as salaries to our workers. There are suppliers who are making demands amounting to three million shillings. So, we need roughly five million shillings to clear most of the pending issues," the manager said.

He doubled up as the chief operations officer of the organization which integrated the finance department. He had every detail about what the organization needed.

"We will deal with the salaries first. I want us to work together to keep the organization running. I know you are aware of what Janet is going through right now," she told him.

"I know some of the things going on. There are also some rumors among the workers. We need to do a lot to keep the organization afloat," he said.

"What rumors?" she asked worried.

"That Janet, our CEO, is a fraudster and a murderer. She was arrested after trying to swindle her insurance off some money and also killing a man who refused to sign the demand notes she had taken him," he said not giving so many details.

"Who started the rumor?" she asked and wished she had not been away from the office for so long.

"It is everywhere. Even the media is discussing it, though they are giving conflicting information. Some are saying that the police are searching for her, others that she has run out of the country, while others are saying she has been arrested but her exact location is unknown. They are saying that effort to reach her lawyers are futile," he explained.

"Please try to control everything. I will be there to shed light on everything tomorrow. I am trying to find out if we can pay the workers by morning tomorrow," Ashley said beginning to get a little depressed.

"That will distract them a bit and will also boost their morale as we try to find out what to do," he said smiling.

He was in desperate need of money. His mistress was pestering him to send her some money to buy herself some new dresses and jewelry. Back home, his wife was expecting him to send some money for the children's medical checkup. His son was complaining of a toothache and the daughter had a problem with her eyesight. The problem was that the national health cover of which he was a faithful contributor did not cover those cases.

"I will get back to you tomorrow. Thank you very much for the information," she said and hung up.

She thought about everything the man had told her. She had to do something to solve the crisis. It was her trying hour and she had to do her best to prove to her friend that she was a reliable person. It would greatly disappoint her if she could not do anything to keep her friend standing even at those trying moments. Though Janet would not expect her to do anything and would even prevent her from doing what she was about to do, she felt it was her duty to make her smile when she was released from prison. She was aware that she did not have the money to pay the workers and that the organization was facing some challenges. In fact, she had been forced to go back into her savings to meet the organization's financial obligations.

"Is it possible to transfer three million shillings just now. I would also request for a loan to top up the balance," she asked the manager when she called him again.

"I am afraid that it might not be possible at the moment. The maximum you can transfer without visiting the bank is one million shillings. I would advise you to visit the bank tomorrow and everything will be sorted out," the bank manager said.

"I have an emergency that cannot wait for that long. Is there not anything you can do?" she asked desperately.

"I am afraid not," he said.

"What do we do now?" she asked almost crying.

She did not want to fail her friend but it seemed like everything was designed to work out her failure. Then she had an idea. Not everything was lost.

Chapter Nineteen

She dialed Rahjeed's number. She could not wait for him. If she did not solve the financial situation with Janet's Foundation, she would never forgive herself. She hoped that it would not take long. If she did not solve the crisis that evening, or at least a part of it, she did not know what would happen the following day.

"Rahjeed, I have to attend to a very urgent matter now. I am afraid I may not wait for you. Let's meet tomorrow," she said.

"Please wait one minute. I am almost there. I am going to take you wherever you are going," he said hastening his steps.

He did not want to miss that moment for anything. He felt that if he did not do it at that time, then he would never get another chance. He wished he had continued with his daily exercises, he would not pant as he was doing then. He felt as if his heart was going to stop any moment.

"What is the problem with you?" Ashley asked at the entrance of the hotel.

He could not speak. He only showed with meaningless signs as he tried to catch his breath. He pointed to the car and made a sign to ask where Ashley was going. She did not understand it but she told him to follow.

"Get into the car if you want to go with me. I don't have much time," she said.

Rahjeed obediently followed her to the car. It was only after twenty minutes that he caught his breath. He looked at her and could not stop admiring her beauty.

"You almost gave me a scare. What is up?" he asked.

"I have to solve a very pressing situation right now. I need some money urgently and I am going to look for it," Ashley said.

"Where are you going to look for it?" he asked looking at his watch.

"Where they keep money. I have to get it before tomorrow," she said.

"It is past seven in the evening, who do you think will help you at this hour?" he asked confused.

"I told you those who keep money," she answered tritely.

"And how much do you need if a may ask?" he asked as if he had a solution.

"Five million shillings, at the present, that is," she said.

"What do you need all that money for?" Rahjeed asked.

"I don't think it is your business to know," she said.

"Maybe I can help," he said.

Ashley parked by the roadside and looked at the man in disbelief. She was wondering where she would get all that money. Her savings were not enough to solve the problem at hand. It would only be enough to cater for the casual workers and some few mid-level workers. She would also be forced to default on her mortgage but that did not matter at that moment. She was thinking of ways to get a loan but her creditworthiness was way below the amount she needed. The banks would not give her the money she needed despite her being a most loyal client for several years.

"Do you know what you are saying? And why would you help me with such amount?" she asked after overcoming the shock and excitement.

"Before I answer your question, there is something I wanted to tell you. I don't know whether this is the appropriate time or not," he said coyly.

"What is it? I told you I don't have time and I have to get the money urgently. So, if it is not about the money, please keep it for some other time," she said in a serious tone.

"It is very important, but not related to your issue," he said fearfully.

"Then keep it for some other time until I resolve my issue. Now back to the funds, I am willing to take a loan from you if you set favorable conditions. And you should know I cannot wait for the funds tomorrow. So, tell me, how much are you willing to loan me," she asked.

"You did not tell me what you need the money for. At least even banks require to be informed about the purpose before they can consider your request, though they do not follow up on it," he said.

"I need to bail out my friend. It is urgent," she said.

"Do you already know where they took her?" he asked shocked.

"It is not about her arrest. Something else more serious," she said.

"Then tell it to me," he said in a serious tone having overcome his earlier fear.

He had realized that he needed to exercise patience if he was going to achieve anything with the girl. He decided to try the next day. Maybe he would be lucky. But he was going to give her the money she needed. He did not need to know what she intended to do with it. He trusted that it was something important to make her get so stressed.

"If I do not get the money by tonight, then Janet's organization risk being closed down and there are creditors threatening to sue her," she said sadly.

"I am going to give you the money. You will give me the details later. Please give me the account to do the wire transfer. It will be done tonight," he said.

"Are you sure?" she asked unwilling to believe.

Why would he do all that for her. Was he not going to ask for at least some form of contract. Why did he follow her wherever she went? For the first time ever since she met him, she started thinking about Rahjeed. She had been so much preoccupied with what was happening to her friend that she had failed to acknowledge the man's presence. It was as if she needed him close to her even though she did not know him. But his action that time made her reflect deeply on a matter she had not thought about. Could he be interested in her?

"Are you giving me the account or not?" he asked, almost in a threatening tone.

"Before I give you the account, I need to know what will be the terms of the loan. I have to know how I am going to meet my obligation after I receive the amount lest I land myself in more trouble," she said enterprisingly.

"I thought you said you have an urgent matter to attend to which cannot go beyond morning, tomorrow. Why are you delaying things?" he asked teasingly.

He was not planning to have her pay back the money. He wanted to help her. Even if she did not accept him in the end, he would be okay. He loved her and wanted to see her happy. Besides, he had so much money that was lying idle in his account. It was time he also started being helpful to the people. He had learned that Janet's foundation was on a worthy course of assisting the less privileged. He could consider the loan as an investment in the cause.

"Consider the money a donation to the organization, just like those who support it to accomplish its goals. We will sign a deal on how I am going to support the organization later," he said businesslike.

Ashley could not believe what she heard. Ever since Janet's troubles started, none of the sponsors of the organization wanted to be associated with her. That was the reason for the financial crisis it was facing. If Rahjeed fulfilled what he was saying, it would be a great boost to its work.

"Okay," she said breathing a sigh of relief.

"Thank you very much," she added.

The transaction was made that night and the following day, the organization was in a position to resume most of its activities. The workers who were angry with Janet and had started rumors against her, even though she had taken them from dirt started a new story of how she was being harassed by the state for her good work to the less privileged. They claimed that some people who wanted to benefit through money laundering were angry with her because she had refused to be used for shady deals.

Though the rumors were unconfirmed, there was some element of truth in it. In fact, that was the real reason she was facing all the problems that she encountered at that moment. They did not know about it though. It seemed everything was conspiring to make her life difficult. The accident was just one of the excuses used to pressure her into accepting her organization to become a conduit of dirty money. Her refusal had been the reason she had fallen out with her father.

The organization was not out of the woods yet. That evening before closing of office, some detectives visited the organization with claims that it was abetting money laundering. They had an order to have it closed down until investigations were completed. Rahjeed was arrested as the mastermind behind the money laundering racket.

"We are going to take you in to answer some few questions at the station," the detectives told him.

They were in Ashley's office where she was filling him in on the operations of the organization. The challenges it had been facing and the pressure from powerful individuals who wanted to use it for their illegal deals.

"What has he done?" she asked furious.

"It is not in your power to know that. He is just going to answer some few questions. If he is innocent, he will be released, if not, then he will have to spend some days at the cells," the detective said laughing raucously.

Ashley did not know how it happened, but she had fallen in love with the guy. She could not wait for him to propose. She regretted having denied him the many chances he had tried to court her. She had thought that after they had settled everything he was going to do it but then they had come and arrested him.

"I am coming with him," Ashley said resolutely.

"We do not need you, woman," the detective said spitefully.

"If he is guilty, then I am as guilty as he is," she said standing by his side.

"That is not upon you to decide. We know our work and I don't think you are going to teach us how to do it," the detective said trying to push her away.

She was adamant. She held onto Rahjeed.

"I will not allow them to take you," she said.

"Don't make matters worse. I will be back within no time. Please take care of things here and then I will call you when I am done at the station," Rahjeed pleaded with her.

"You don't know these people. They are going to take you as they did Janet. Who are they going to leave me with?" she asked almost crying.

The words deeply touched Rahjeed. They gave him the strength to face whatever was coming ahead. He looked at her and loved her even the more.

"It is nothing, I promise you. I am going to be back within no time," he said.

"Within no time, foolish man," the detective said in his heart.

"Madam, allow us to do our work or we are going to have you charged for obstruction of justice," he added.

"It is okay. Just let them do what they are doing. We cannot be the ones to break the law," Rahjeed said pensively.

Ashley reluctantly allowed the officers to take Ranjeet. She sat on her chair wondering what was going on. After they had gone she remembered she needed to call Janet's lawyer. Probably they were going to add more charges on her sheet. She was not sure which forces they were fighting with and who they would take next. Maybe they would go for her.

"Hello, they have just arrested Rahjeed," Ashley told Janet's lawyer over the phone.

"Why and where did they take him?" she asked from the other end.

She had tried all she could to trace Janet to no avail. No judge was willing to help her and it seemed as if the media houses had also been recruited into the ring. They were not reporting what was happening. She tried calling some of her friends who were reporters to cover the story but they all declined.

"You know this is a very sensitive case involving a very powerful man. Everyone has been paid to silence and if I try to bring it up, my life will be in danger. Besides, the editor will not allow me even to begin working on it," a lady reporter who was her friend told her.

"So, everyone is going to keep quiet as these atrocities go on before our eyes?" she asked desperately.

"We have no choice. Everyone who tries to do good in this part of the world just signs a death sentence. It is just that way. You know how many people have disappeared mysteriously for harboring the truth they should not have accessed in the first place or showing kindness when they were not supposed to, or even not being able to participate in the wisdom acts of 'when you get the opportunity, eat as much as you can because you never know what tomorrow might bring'. It is a dire situation but we have to accept things as they are," the reporter told her.

She realized she would have to fight for her client alone. As it were, it appeared she was headed for death even without trial. She had witnessed many of such cases to begin fooling herself. She did not understand what Janet could have done to make her a target of such magnitude. She knew there were powerful and corrupt individuals behind the case and she too needed to trend carefully.

"Where are you?" the lawyer asked Ashley.

"I am at the office," she answered depressed.

"Stay there and ask the guards not to allow anyone in until I come," she told Ashley.

Chapter Twenty

Skunka introduced Lennington to the judge who was going to preside over the cases he was presenting. He was bound to win the cases and all the parties, except those being represented, would benefit and celebrate their success.

Skunka was a calculating and scheming man who had made a fortune for himself when others were languishing in poverty. Many of his mates during the times he was in government were struggling to make ends meet. He made it a point not to disclose his secret of doing business to anyone. He had understood that in order to evade the wheels of justice, you had to be as big and as loaded to make the grease that made them roll work in your favor.

"Skunka, what do you want this time? I thought you already had enough," the judge asked welcoming them to his study.

"Has it ever been enough? If you have not had enough, then you should know I have not even started getting what I should. How can you say I have had enough when I have not even made it into the list of the wealthiest people of my countrymen, and yet I aspire a position in the world?" Skunka asked.

"You are always aggressive and never get enough. Hope one day it will not catch up with you and make you lose everything," the judge said.

"As long as I am getting everything, there is no way I am going to lose everything, justice Mikima. You taught me as much yourself. You also taught me to know my circles so I don't end up shedding my sweat for nothing. It is you who taught me there is nothing like justice, at least not as defined by the common men. You taught me that justice is when one had made others surrender what they have and worship you instead. As long as one has not reached there, then justice has not been achieved and it is one's goal to reach it. It has nothing to do with others, but has everything to do with one's interests. Others are just objects to be used to achieve those personal goals of justice," Skunka said proudly.

"So, what do you want? What sort of justice do you want to accomplish this time and why have you brought another?" Justice Mikima asked.

"As you advised me earlier, whenever I see a man who has the potential to keep one company as they seek for their personal justice and rise to the top, I should not dump that man but establish what they have and how we can work it out together for the good of all those who deserve it at the top. Meet lawyer Lennington, he knows how to play the game, albeit, on his own learning. He can learn and do more if he is under the tutelage of someone experienced. Lennington, meet justice Mikima. Be free to learn and welcome to the club," Skunka said introducing them to each other.

"Thank you," Lennington said coyly.

He was still anxious about everything. If anything went wrong, it would be the end of him, but if all worked according to plan, he would join the league of the most accomplished men in the society.

After a few pleasantries, Lennington explained the nature of the cases. Justice Mikima was more than impressed. It had been long since he landed such an important job. He would do it with all the dedication.

The case took approximately two years. During the period, Janet was in and out of remand. She would get of one remand and then get into another. It was like the jailers were having an exchange program or they needed her to learn about the state of every facility in the country.

She had given up hope in life and just wanted to die. She did not know what they wanted with her and all efforts by her lawyer to have her released according to the law were futile. They all waited for what would happen. Her organization had been closed indefinitely and there were no hopes it was going to be running again. The workers had all left and only a shell of it was left.

As for Rahjeed, the authorities fought a hard battle to have him deported, but it seemed his lawyers were strong and the judge on his case incorruptible. That, added to Ashley's prayers, perhaps worked to keep him in the country. They did what they could to help Janet, but they were too small to be of any significance. So, they just waited.

One evening, three days before Janet's case about the accident was determined, Rahjeed asked Ashley out. Earlier in the day, they had been prevented from visiting Janet in her cell. No reason had been given for it. The warden just said:

"She cannot be visited at the moment."

"But why?" Ashley had tried to protest.

"Just go by the fact that she cannot be visited and be content with that. If you press too hard, you might find yourself joining her. You know there are many crimes that might be placed on you. They are always ready, by the way, waiting for someone to carry them," the warden had said in a subtle threat.

She had received orders from her boss that Janet should not be visited. She could not question that. All she could do was obey the orders or find herself jobless or even worse. She chose to keep her job and not find out the worst that could happen.

"Are you ready for a dinner out?" Rahjeed asked after they had stayed one hour in the house.

They had both moved in at Janet's, though they stayed in different rooms. Rahjeed had yet to propose to Ashley and was afraid it was taking too long. He wished he could stop everything and tell her how much he loved her.

"Is there any need? I just feel bored and hopeless about everything. I think we made a mistake to be born here," Ashley said downhearted.

"You can't lose hope like that. Maybe the fact that you were born here was to be able to do something and bring hope to many like you who would be helpless and hopeless to do a thing," he told her.

"Where do you want us to go?" she asked without showing any interest.

She did not want to disappoint the man who had shown her nothing but kindness. Since the whole thing started, she felt like she was in a nightmare that was never going to end. She felt that she had failed her friend terribly. She could not keep her organization running and she could not do anything to get her free.

"I think I better make it a surprise. You should cheer up. Everything is going to be well," he said as he took her hand.

She did not resist. She followed him without saying a thing. Whatever he wanted, she would follow. At least if only to please him.

"We are here already," he said as he opened the door for her.

She stepped out of the vehicle and followed him to a dull lit room at the end of the restaurant, reserved only for two. She looked at him and then at the room. Though she understood what that meant, she was not ready for it at that moment.

"Are you sure about this?" she asked.

"About what?" he asked her.

"I thought it was going to be a simple dinner. Maybe something to help us relax our minds after everything that has happened. But it seems you have other ideas," she said.

"I thought it was important to celebrate my release and also help you overcome some of the stress. That is why I chose this place," he said.

"I don't think it was necessary," she said disinterestedly.

"There is something else I wanted to say. I think this is the ideal place to do that," he added.

Ashley did not have the energy to argue. She followed him into the room ready to listen to what he was going to say. She knew she was going to disappoint him, but she would do her best to make it easy on him.

"Ashley, I have been holding this for too long. I wanted that we be the two of us when I did this," he said removing a box from his pocket.

They were waiting for their order to be served as he made the proposal. His heart was racing. He did not know how to do it better. He did not know whether to do it before, during or after dinner, but when he realized that the order would take thirty minutes to be ready, he could not wait.

"Rahjeed, I am not saying no. Please stand and listen to what I have to say," she said in a serious tone.

Rahjeed felt like a knife had been dug into his chest. He had been so hopeful that he had not seen her rejecting him at all. He looked at her still thinking she was teasing him, like she was testing him.

"Please stand and don't take this wrongly. I love you but we need some time. At this moment, it would feel like I am betraying my friend if I went ahead with this. Though you know what the answer is, can we wait after she is out? I would wish she were present during my engagement," she said trying to be as kind as she could.

"I will wait for as much as is necessary. I am only hoping it will not be too long," he said as he returned the box into the pocket.

He had waited for two years, just a little longer would not be too much. It was not going to be easy though, but he understood where she was coming from and he respected her.

They took their dinner in silence and left the hotel shortly afterwards. Though they had so much to talk about, it seemed as if it could not be expressed in words. Both of them hoped and wished the case would be done with and their lives would be restored to them.

Chapter Twenty One

After leaving Justice Mikima's study, they drove to Skunka's study. He said that he had something important to tell him. It was as if Lennington had become his confidant but there was something about him he felt he could not trust. He had to be careful before him. With such men, things could topple any minute and without notice.

"What is it that you wanted to tell me? I need to go and prepare for the accident case," he said impatiently.

"I have another deal that will be between you and me. It is going to involve killing someone to get it done though and I need you to be discreet about it as much as possible," he said checking from side to side as if someone was listening.

"Why should someone get killed? I think the case is straightforward and will go as the judge promised us," Lennington asked.

"The money involved can only be released upon the death of that person. It is someone involved in the case. The amount of money involved is so much that the proceeds from all your cases will look like peanuts in comparison. I only need you to organize the elimination, and of course your discretion," Skunka said in a serious tone.

"This is a serious thing and very risky. We have to be very careful about everything," Lennington said worried.

He had not thought it would get to that. He could be everything but not a murderer. Whatever Skunka was proposing was out of the question. He did not think he would do it, but still Skunka was not a man to play games with. The fact that he had disclosed the plan to him meant he was also in line of those who would be taken out if he did not agree to what he was suggesting. He was in a dilemma.

"Is it really necessary to have the person die? Is there no other way?" he asked.

"Unfortunately, there is none. It is a life insurance compensation, and as you are aware, such can only be settled upon the death of the insured. If you understand what I mean," Skunka said.

Lennington got the point. The only thing he did not understand was why he was disclosing that to him. He wished he had left him only with the cases, whatever he would get would be enough for him. He was not asking for more.

"And who is the person in question?" he asked.

"I will disclose the identity later. For now, I will give you some contacts you are going to use for the purpose," Skunka told him.

"Why me? What will you do?" he asked getting even more agitated.

"I can't get involved, otherwise, everything would be futile. No one should even suspect I am part of the plan. That is why only you should plan everything and you have to be careful not to get caught. You will get your part, a very generous portion that you will never have to work again for the rest of your life," Skunka said.

"Why do I feel like you are exaggerating things?" he asked.

"I would not exaggerate such an important issue. When are you going to do it?" Skunka asked.

"I am not sure about it. I think the whole thing is too risky and you should think about abandoning it," Lennington said.

"That is not possible. You have to go ahead with the plan and you cannot look back. I know you want money and now that you have joined the club, you could as well get yourself ready to get involved in any activity it carries out. You have come too far to look back," Skunka said warning him.

"Then fill me on everything and then help me with the plan. You know I have never been involved in such before," Lennington said, realizing there was no way out.

Skunka explained to him everything that needed to be done. He had already organized the men who were going to carry out the execution. Lennington was to be the client who would order it.

He went from the house a frightened man. He wished he had never involved himself in any of the plans of these men. Whatever Skunka had told him was too sensitive he did not see it fit to share it with his friend. He would go ahead with it and inform him of it later. If he made a mistake, he would have to deal with the consequences.

*   *   *

"My lord, my client cannot be judged for something she was not in control of. When the accident happened, she had no way of avoiding the man who jumped onto the road from nowhere. On the insurance cover, she cannot be judged for the fall of the insurance company. She is a victim of corporate negligence for which she needs to be compensated as well. I rest my case," Janet's lawyer said.

Lennington stood smiling. He already knew what was going to happen, but he still had to make his case anyway. He approached Janet who stood there like a zombie. She had given up about everything and whatever was going to happen, she was ready for it.

"My lord. This is murder and pure negligence. This woman here knows it is a crime to drive a vehicle without a valid license. My clients were robbed of their son because of a careless driver who did not care about road rules. The son of my client was walking calmly on the pedestrian walk when a driver who thought owning a car gave them a right to despise those who walk on the road hit him. He was a promising young man who had a whole future ahead of him, but now he is no more because of a careless driver who does not value life. For that, I make a prayer to the court to give her the life sentence, what is fit for a murderer.

I am also praying that the court orders the murderer…"

"Objection you honor, I ask my learned friend to withdraw that statement. My client is not a murderer and the court has not found her guilty of anything," Janet's lawyer stood.

"Objection sustained. Please refrain yourself from using such terms," the judge instructed.

"I rephrase the statement my lord. As I was saying, this woman here has killed an innocent man because of her negligence. On top of it, she did not see it fit to have a valid insurance. I pray the court to order her to compensate the family of the client as would have been the case with an insurance company. I rest my case," Lennington said and sat smiling like one who had already won the case.

"I will give the decision of the court in the afternoon. The court is adjourned," the judge ordered.

During the recess, Lennington made several calls. Whatever he was supposed to do was to be done that day. The men were ready and were waiting for his instructions. Everything had to be done precisely.

"All rise, justice Mikima presiding," the clerk said when the court went back in session.

"After listening to both sides of the case and the testimonies of the witnesses, the court has come up with the following verdict.

On the first account, the court finds the accused guilty of careless driving and killing a pedestrian and sentences her to ten years in prison. On the second count, the court finds the accused guilty of driving without a valid insurance. Even though she was not in control of what was happening with the insurance company under which the car was insured, she was supposed to find out if the insurance certificate she was holding would be valid before taking the vehicle on the road. In this regard, the court orders her to compensate the family of the client with one million shillings. You have fourteen days to appeal against the court's judgement. Court dismissed."

After the verdict, Kahiga analyzed everything and thought there was an injustice that was about to be carried out. He did not think his family needed the compensation the judge was talking about. Besides, he was beginning to lose trust with Lennington, the family lawyer. Even though they had signed the contract with him, he was feeling that the family needed a way to cancel the contract.

He felt he needed to do something that would protect an innocent person from injustice. He would make things right even if it meant losing compensation for the family.

He approached Ashley. He had observed everything and it seemed like she was a sister to the accused. He would propose to her the desire to drop the case. He would talk with his mother about it later but he had to do something that was going to restore faith in humanity. He would not just sit back and allow injustice to take place as he watched.

"Excuse me, madam, would you mind giving me twenty minutes afterwards. There is something important I want to tell you, but I want to talk to my lawyer first," Kahiga told Ashley as they were getting out of the courtroom.

"No problem. Where do we meet? He will accompany me," she said referring to Rahjeed.

"No problem. You could come with Janet's lawyer if possible. I sense something sinister going on and I don't think it is fair to allow it to continue," Kahiga said wondering how to explain it to them.

He was afraid they would not even listen to him. They were facing against each other but after the entire case, he had realized whom they were all facing against.

"Okay, we will be waiting for you," Ashley said hopefully.

Whatever was going to help her friend she was ready to do. Even if it meant bowing to the enemy, she would do it. She did not know why her instinct told her that this man provided a glimmer of hope for her friend. Normally, she would not have allowed the man to talk leave alone agreeing to talk with him.

"They are taking her to the women's prison now. We have already talked with the police manning the vehicle. There will be no problem. They will give a signal at intersection eight. Be ready and do a clean job. I will be waiting for your report," Lennington said and hung up.

Kahiga pretended that he had not heard anything. He approached him as if he was in a hurry. He was right all along; the man was a swindler and a criminal. He was not even certain his family was going to get any cent of what the court had awarded them.

"How long have you been here?" Lennington said assessing if yet another soul needed to be taken away from the earth.

"I have just arrived. Now that the cases are over, how long are we going to wait for the family to receive the compensation values?" Kahiga asked.

"About your father, it will take utmost two months to have the funds released to the family. They will be released through me as your lawyer. As for your wife, I am looking at somewhere between five to twelve months if anything goes well. And as for your brother, it depends on whether they are going to make any appeal. But it should not take long, say five or six months. I will keep you updated," Lennington said as if he was trying to dismiss him.

"And the same case applies to your village mate. What was her name?" he asked as if he had remembered something very important.

"Phyllis," Kahiga answered.

He had known he had also taken her case, and with all the cases won, he would be swimming in cash. He doubted he was going to give any of the families the money they had won.

"What do I need to do?" Kahiga asked.

"I will call you. Just keep your line on and then I will keep you informed about the progress," Lennington said.

"There was something I also wanted to find out," Kahiga said intending to find out what would happen to Janet.

"What is it?" Lennington said impatiently.

This man was wasting his time. He did not want to lose time. Within a month, he would be far away and they would search for him but would not find him. It was good they had agreed to do business with him, but as it were, the circles he had joined did not care about feelings. Too bad they would not even get the few thousands he was planning to give them. Others would get the compensation, they had gotten the injuries and the scars; they could allow others to get the money. After all, was not sharing advised among all religions.

"Is there a way that woman can be saved from the jail term and the compensation from her forfeited?" he asked pensively.

"Don't worry about that. All you desire is going to happen, maybe faster than you imagine," Lennington said with a chuckle.

"Thank you very much, I need to get going," Kahiga said keeping in mind the location he had Lennington say over the phone.

"I will keep you updated," he shouted from behind.

"You fool, he said to himself.

Kahiga approached one of the officers close by. He wanted to learn something about the prisoners who were being transported. His heart told him he needed to do something to protect the innocent woman whom everybody accused of killing his brother. It appeared the lawyer was planning something against her, not just made her face injustice from the system.

Chapter Twenty Two

"I am sorry to bother you. I think we have to do something to save Janet. We cannot allow them to take her from here," Kahiga ran to Ashley after leaving Lennington.

"What are you talking about?" Ashley asked confused and worried.

"I think they are planning something evil against her. I overheard my lawyer calling someone. I am not so sure what they were talking about, but they said the prisoner will be ambushed on intersection eight. The problem is that we cannot trust anyone here and so we cannot report anything to anyone. He said he has already talked with the officers accompanying her to prison and they are the ones to give the signal. If we allow them to take her from here, we may never know what they will do to her. The lawyer is a criminal who has made a name by swindling others. They win their cases by buying judges," Kahiga explained.

"What do you suggest we do?" Rahjeed asked.

"I think we should distract them as they are taking her out of the courtroom. We will snatch her from their arms before they can take her anywhere. It is going to be a risky business but I don't see any other way," Kahiga said concerned.

"And why are you so willing to help us? How do we know that you can be trusted?" Rahjeed asked.

"I don't think we have time for that. We could be endangering her life as we speak. Let's just say I want to end an injustice. More details will come later please. Let's do the most urgent thing first. She will be taken out of the courtroom any time. If they leave with her, we might not be able to save her," Kahiga said.

He had developed a new resolve. Ever since his wife was taken ill and what he went through trying to get her treatment, the cases and his interaction with the lawyer, he had come to learn so many things about the system. He decided to carry out his own investigations into several matters that led him to the decision to do something to stop the evil that was being propagated in the land and making many people suffer. No one as yet knew what he had found out but he meant to do something against injustice and corruption.

"What are you talking about?" Janet's lawyer asked from behind them.

Kahiga took her away in a polite way and explained everything he had learned. He told her about Janet and requested her to ask her friends to help her. He knew what he was suggesting was illegal, but it was the only available option.

"I understand and I am willing to help," she said as they joined the rest.

"I am a lawyer and I have established that if we don't do something radical, injustice will continue to reign in the land. We can't allow this situation to continue. For instance, what happened inside there was bogus but there is nothing anyone can do. They have already planned everything to work according to their interests and even appealing to a higher court will yield nothing. And then, after what you have told me, we won't even get the chance to appeal," she added.

"Are you so easily convinced by this man? What makes him think we can trust him yet he was part of the people who are making Janet's life a living hell?" Rahjeed asked tired by everything that was happening.

Everything looked like fiction and he wondered if he would ever get back to reality. Maybe the only real thing about all that was happening was Ashley. She was the only one he wished to remember from the entire nightmare. He had never thought in his life he would step in a police cell, he did in a weirdest of ways.

"We don't have time to argue. I want you to incite some people and start a demo outside the courtroom. As they try to disperse you and the people who will be willing to join us, Kahiga will whisk Janet away. If we don't do that, they are going to kill her," the lawyer said.

"Is it that serious?" Ashley asked shaken.

"Yes, it is, and if we don't do something fast we are going to lose her. Who knows who among us they will go for next. Living in this land is becoming so dangerous and it appears whatever effort one is making, they are securing their own death," the lawyer said.

"When do we do that?" Rahjeed asked looking at Kahiga suspiciously.

"Take this. Gather a few and pay them. As they take Janet out, gather around with the people chanting anti-injustice slogans and Kahiga will be waiting at the exit waiting to strike. I will tell you where to meet when everything is done. Is there any question?" the lawyer explained taking a bundle of notes from her handbag.

"I will add some more if it is going to help our friend," Rahjeed said.

"There is more I think we need to talk about. You still have questions to answer. And don't dare do any harm to Janet. Understand?" Rahjeed told Kahiga.

They went around the compound and the area outside the court as fast as they could and gathered a number of idle youths. They then gathered outside the courtroom as if they were waiting for their case to start. No one had ever witnessed such a calm crowd.

Fifteen minutes later, Janet walked outside slowly. Her hands were handcuffed and she looked totally wretched. Her hair was tied in three ugly braids and her complexion had changed a great deal. Despite her state, her beauty still glowed and many men outside the courtroom drooled as they watched her being taken away.

"What a waste," one of the men commented.

Before they could get to the car, the crowd that stood calmly started pushing forward unexpectedly taking the officers by surprise. In the mix, Kahiga whisked Janet and rushed towards her lawyer's waiting car. She did not even get a chance to react.

The officers who were guarding her shot in the air to disperse the crowds as the car sped towards the open gate breaking the barrier and speeding off towards the road outside town. Two men were shot dead in the process. Ashley's ankle was injured and she could not walk.

"Ashley, what is the problem?" Rahjeed asked when the situation had calmed down.

"I have hurt my ankle," she replied.

"Officer, what is going on? Please help me take this woman to safety," Rahjeed asked feigning ignorance.

"Is that woman not your friend? Who wants so much to destroy her?" the officer asked as he helped Rahjeed take Ashley to the car.

"I don't know what they want with her or what she has done to deserve that. Even the worst enemy of the state does not go through what she has faced," Rahjeed answered as they reached their car.

"Where have they taken her now and why could they not allow her to be taken to the women prison calmly? She was not showing any resistance," Rahjeed asked.

"I don't know what is happening, but it appears that your friend messed with a very powerful person. They never allow anyone who messes with them to live. Pray that they do not kill her," the officer told him.

"What do you mean?" Rahjeed asked.

"I overheard at the canteen that they are going to whip her off, that she cannot be allowed to live. I did not get most of the details, but it appears that she has messed with a very important person who does not want her to continue living," the officer said.

"Thank you very much. Let me take her to hospital. I will look for you one day for a cup of coffee," Rahjeed said handing him one thousand shillings note.

Meanwhile, several men were arrested for causing disturbance. Most of them were released the following day with fines from five hundred shillings to one thousand shillings. None of them understood what they were protesting about. They only did as they were instructed for a mere two hundred shillings. They could not even point out who had paid them.

"Do you think they are going to harm her? I hope they are not going to catch up with them. I hope she will be safe," Ashley asked as they drove towards a private clinic belonging to Rahjeed's friend.

"Don't worry, everything is going to be well. We will soon be with your friend, our friend," he assured her.

"How is your ankle?" he asked.

"It is hurting too much. But, can we go to her? I want to be with her. Did you see how she looked? Why are they doing this to her?" Ashley said crying.

"We have to get your ankle treated first and then find out where they went. They will call us as soon as they are somewhere safe," Rahjeed told her.

"They are taking too long to call. Can you call them?" she asked.

"It is not wise to do that. Let's have you treated first. I know they will have called before the doctor completes the treatment," Rahjeed said.

"Okay. But make sure she is safe. I will only answer to your proposal when she is safe. You have to assure me you are going to ensure she is safe," Ashley said resolutely.

"Don't worry, I will make sure that she is safe. We have to leave everything in the hands of God though. Pray that He protects her. He is the only one who can keep her safe," he told her.

"She has to be well. Nothing can happen to her. I promised to always be with her and I can't fail her now," she said hysterically.

"It is going to be well," he told her comfortingly.

"How can you talk so casually? Do you know what she means to me? Do you have any idea what she is going through? Did you look at her? She is so worn out and emaciated. I need to be with her. Please take me to her. I want to be with her," Ashley cried out.

Rahjeed realized he was not going to achieve anything trying to assure her. She was so depressed and she needed to relax. He opened a compartment on the dashboard and as she cried, he injected her with a sedative that sent her to sleep in a minute.

Chapter Twenty Three

The unexpected commotion at the court house gave them enough time to lose the authorities. Before the officers could react and make necessary communication, they had reached the first intersection. They took a rarely used road and changed cars. Within the short time they communicated with Kahiga, Janet's efficient lawyer had organized a runaway car and made sure they could not be easily traced.

"Don't worry. You are safe now," the lawyer told the shaken Janet.

"Where are you taking me? Are you a part of them?" she asked her in a resigned tone of voice.

She had gone through the worst a human could go through in life and just wanted to die. They had tortured her in the cells and done the most debased things in those cells which made her lose her worth as a human. She did not trust anyone. It was like everyone had turned to her enemy.

"No, we want to help you. They wanted to kill you but you are now safe," the lawyer said shocked.

She did not know Janet like that. The Janet she knew was a lively woman who was very focused about life. An energetic lady who motivated others to action. The Janet she was with now was weak and shaken to the core. She looked like one who did not have hope in life and even acted like she did not know her. What had they done to her? She knew she had failed her as her lawyer, but she had tried her best.

"Why did you not allow them to kill me? I just want to die. I have nothing to live for," she said weakly.

"What are you talking about? You have so much to live for and we are going to help you to find yourself once again. They may have tried to break you but you are going to rise again stronger," she tried to comfort her.

"And who is this man? I think I have seen him somewhere. Yes. Sorry for killing your brother. I did not mean to do it. It was just an accident," she said.

"It is okay. Don't worry about anything. I am here to help you. I am Kahiga," he said trying to encourage her.

"Why are you not angry with me? I took away your brother from you. You should allow me to get the punishment," she said.

"Don't worry about that. As you said, it was just an accident," Kahiga said trying as much as possible to comfort her.

"Or you want to kill me to avenge him? I am ready to die. I am ready to pay for my sins and if you feel that killing me will give the punishment faster and better than a jail term, I am ready to take it, only don't make it too painful. I have gone through a lot of pain as it were," she said resignedly.

"No one here is going to kill you. We are going to help you. Sorry about everything you have gone through. We are victims of a wicked system and we can only support one another to overcome the system. We cannot allow things to get worse than this," Kahiga said.

"I don't understand what you are saying. I need to rest," she said and lay back on the chair and closed her eyes.

"Will she ever get her life back?" Kahiga asked.

"When everything is settled, I will get her the best therapist. She is going to be well," the lawyer said hopefully.

"I believe she is going to get well," he said as he watched her sleeping.

They drove to a remote village about four hundred kilometers from town. Lawyer Damaris had talked to one of her clients whom she had helped win a case against a powerful politician who had defiled her when she went seeking for help from him. The lady had invited Nina to her place and had even adopted her as her own daughter despite being five years older than her. Her husband had not objected to it and therefore Damaris became as one of the children of that family. She often visited them whenever she had time or when she wanted to relax.

"Oh Damaris, you have come. I can see you have brought some more visitors," the lady was excited to see her.

She lived in a little mud house. Several huts surrounded the house. It was where her children slept. Thanks to Nina, she had taken all of them to schools in town. They were there at that moment.

"Would you mind if we spent some weeks here. These are my friends, Janet, she is feeling unwell; and this is Kahiga," she said in a request.

"You know this is your home. You can stay for as long as you want," the lady told her.

"Thank you very much. Kahiga, we are going to hide here for the time being. No one will be able to find us here. Hope you will be comfortable. The huts are not like the houses in town, they don't have nice beds but they will serve us for the moment," she said in a language the lady did not understand.

"No problem. I am used to all sorts of situations," Kahiga said.

Damaris and Janet took one hut and Kahiga was taken to a separate one. They found a way of breaking the handcuffs and freed Janet's hands. Later that evening, they talked about the injustices and the corrupt systems that were making people suffer. They vowed to bring the change that was needed. They would bring the health system to where it was supposed to be and deal with the rogue insurance companies that were only concerned with giving the last sendoff compensation with little care about the health they claimed to insure.

*　　*　　*

"She has escaped," Lennington said over the phone.

"How could she escape? You have to find her and do as we had agreed. I can't lose all that money," Skunka said furiously.

"I did my best and now I have to run and keep under for some time. My clients will start looking for me to get their settlements according to the court rulings. I need to be as far away as possible. All the best with their quest to get the claim," Lennington said pompously.

"Do you think you can run away from me?" Skunka asked.

"I have done my part and even though I have not accomplished the last part, that was none of my business. I think I am content with what I have received. As you can see, I am not a bad man. I have wired the shares of each of the people involved to your accounts. If you mind to check, you will find your share complete as we agreed," Lennington said.

"You are playing with fire. You should be aware that I have networks everywhere and no one hides from me. I have given you twenty-four hours.

133

If you will not have finished the task by then, you will know that they did not call me Skunka for nothing," Skunka threatened.

"All the best Skunka. It was nice doing business with you. I have to go now," Lennington said and hung up.

Two strange men boarded the light plane he had taken to the neighboring country of South Sudan. He knew he could plan from there anything that he needed to do to settle his life. He had accumulated enough and as he had promised, he was going to change his life and would stop swindling people of their insurance claims. The money he had gathered was enough to help him start lucrative businesses. He would even begin going to church and helping in charity work.

Before takeoff, the strange men exited the light plane. It was strange but Lennington did not think much about it. It was good that they were giving him the space to himself. How favorable could fate be towards him.

The plane took off at four in the evening. At an office a few meters from the airport, a man smiled in his office. He was glad that whatever he did always succeeded. He had come to believe that people without a heart always did well in everything they put their hands to.

"Goodbye my friend. You have just secured your death," the man said pulling heavily on his cigar and blowing the smoke towards the plane that was picking attitude fast.

Just at that moment, a blast was heard from the ground. It shook the entire building and it came down crumbling like it was made of straw. The sky was filled with dust and smoke as authorities, reporters and members of the public surrounded the place to find what was going on.

A few moments later, media reports were awash with news of a terrorist group claiming responsibility for the act. Several high-ranking government officials who had offices in the building were reported missing.

Meanwhile, the plane that Lennington had boarded developed mechanical problems just a moment before it entered South Sudan airspace. The cabin filled with smoke and the engines failed, the plane crashed killing all the passengers. It burst into flames and the spot in the forested border where it crashed resembled hell.

Chapter Twenty Four

Ashley woke up feeling delighted and hopeful about life. The past several months had been hell but the silver lining of their dark cloud seemed to be approaching. They were finally going to relax from the troubles of systems they thought they knew and understood, but which they discovered they knew nothing about.

"So, Kahiga, you think if each one of us did their part and was brave enough to work out the change they desire we would be able to turn the tables and make the systems work for us instead of the other way round?" Damaris asked as Ashley joined them in the living room.

"What are you talking about?" Ashley asked.

"Oh, you are awake? Your sweetheart was asking for you, he can't wait for the wedding to take place," Damaris said ushering Ashley to a cup of tea.

"And where is he now?" she asked.

"He is decorating the venue of the reception. I wish you people should have prepared a big party. You all deserve it," Damaris said.

"Hope you have not changed your mind, Kahiga? Why are you not helping Rahjeed? If you don't go through with it, then start thinking about what you are going to tell Rahjeed. I am also going to call it off immediately," Ashley threatened.

"What are you going to call off?" Janet asked rubbing her eyes.

"Oh, you are also awake honey? Hope you have not changed your mind?" Kahiga asked going to hug her.

"And why should I change my mind? Is there something that I need to know that you haven't told me? I will cancel everything immediately, but you are going to compensate me for wasting me and giving me false hopes. My lawyer is here," Janet said kissing him on the cheek.

"Can you people stop joking about serious things. My mother used to tell me that whenever you are organizing an important activity, it is not good to joke about it. It attracts bad luck," Damaris said.

"Oh, we don't want to attract bad luck. No one will joke about the day anymore. And as we are on it, when are you going to show us your man?" Janet asked her going to hug her.

"Oh, yes. How sweet would it be if we had three weddings at the same time," Ashley said joining Janet in hugging the lawyer who had been with them through thick and thin.

"And who said she doesn't have a man. You know, when a man finds his ways and reverts from their evil, they also find their destiny. Do you think I was going to be left behind in this transformation?" Justice Mikima shouted from the door.

"What?" Janet and Ashley left Damaris' embrace and tried to overcome the shock.

Kahiga and Damaris were the only ones composed at that moment. It was as if Kahiga knew what was going on.

"Why were we kept in the dark?" Janet demanded.

"When did it all begin?" Ashley asked.

"I am a lawyer," Damaris said smiling.

"And I am a judge," Justice Mikima added.

"And we take our oaths seriously," they said in unison.

"Someone should get Rahjeed here. What is he doing outside? We cannot be concerned about celebrations. Our work is just beginning. We have to bring a change in the systems one step at a time until we bring all the people to experience the dignity of life," Justice Mikima said.

Ashley rushed out and came dragging, literally, Rahjeed from outside.

"How can you be getting involved in petty things when there are serious things to discuss? Do you want me to cancel the wedding?" she asked as she made him to sit and sat on his lap.

"We said no joking about it, Ashley. I am going to fine you one hundred thousand shillings. You are going to sponsor the party this evening," Damaris said pointing at Ashley.

"But how can you fine me? You don't have the authority as yet," she said defensively but apologized all the same.

"I am a judge now and can make the orders. I have added another thirty thousand shillings for contempt," Damaris said seriously.

"Where am I going to get all that money?" she asked feigning shock.

"And what am I here for?" Rahjeed asked kissing her lightly on the lips.

"There is something I want to know. If we are going to have three weddings, and Justice Mikima was supposed to be the one officiating the weddings, who is going to do it for you Damaris and Mikima," Janet asked.

"Who said Mikima is qualified to officiate any union? Do you want everything to be null?" a tall man in his early sixties said from the door.

"And who is this?" Janet asked.

The day was turning out to be full of surprises. For the first time in a long time, she felt she was alive. She sat on Kahiga's lap and waited for the man to introduce himself.

Kahiga stood there dazed. What was his father in law doing there at that moment? He had been the one who advised him to go ahead with the wedding. They had discussed several things, including the children. As he thought about it, he wondered where his mother could be. Why was she taking so long to bring the children? Janet had accepted them immediately and they had all fallen in love with her. She was the perfect woman to be their mother. Though she could not replace their mother, they had accepted her and loved her like they would have their mother. They could not wait for the wedding to start living together.

Uncle Sam had been a judge of the high court for ten years. He was a respected man who always ensured justice was served to all. He had helped many families against oppression by the state systems. He wished he could make people come to their senses.

"Kahiga, I am going to fine you," uncle Sam said smiling as he took his chair.

"I think Janet will give me a higher fine. Meet my father, everyone calls him uncle Sam," Kahiga said apologetically.

"What? You are a liar. You told m…"

"Yes, it is true. I did not get the chance to introduce you to the father of my late wife, Jennifer," Kahiga said kissing Janet on the forehead.

"Nice to meet you father," Janet said shyly as she greeted the man.

"Justice Samuel Mbatu is going to officiate the weddings. Anyone with an objection to that?" Justice Mikima asked.

"No," they all answered.

"Father, don't say you are throwing us away and denying us our mother?" the children shouted as they led their grandmother into the room.

"How can we forget you? Come and join us here," Janet said creating room for them.

"Even you mother," she said as she made a place for the old woman.

"Okay, before we continue, we are going to sign a pact to protect our people. We are going to stop murder in our land. Those who work cannot be working hard to secure their death. We need to secure life and make it more meaningful for all people. We must restore dignity. Anyone who is not willing to be part of this pact can as well drop out of the unions we are going to officiate here," uncle Sam said.

He removed some documents from his briefcase and gave each one of them a copy. Even the children got their copies, and the old woman as well. They all committed to working towards a just society.

The three couples, uncle Sam, Kahiga's mother and the children tossed after the couples had signed their marriage certificates.

"TO LIFE AND DIGNITY, FOREVER." They shouted as they celebrated a new dawn that would be worked out by them.

The end